I0412702

Vitruvian Quality

Peter Leeson

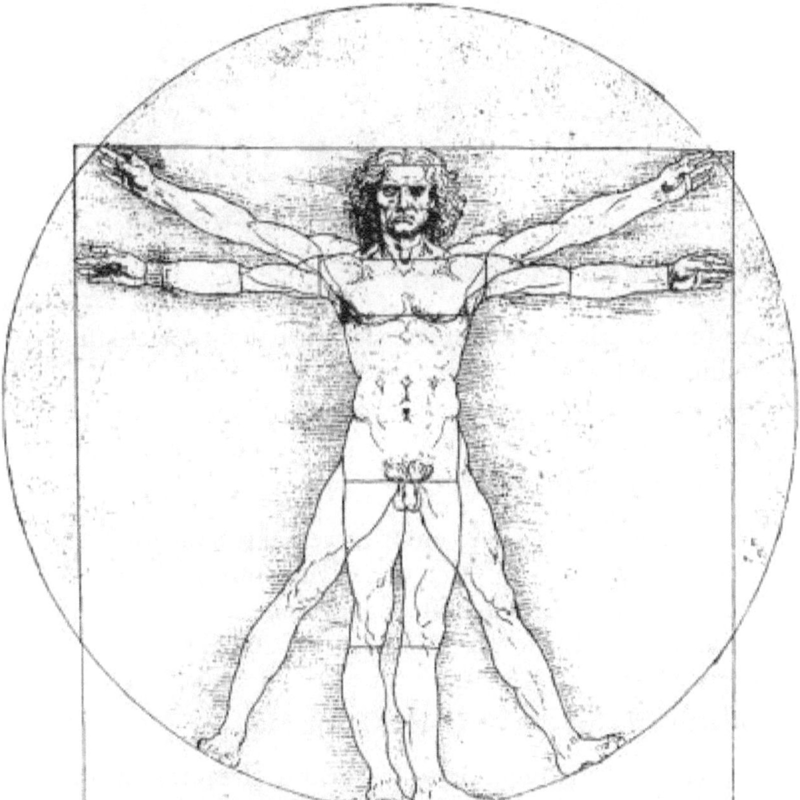

Getting your docs in a row

ISBN 978-1-4710-6753-2

By the same author

Orchestrated Knowledge

An introduction to a business structure that replaces the traditional hierarchy with a knowledge network.
Orchestrated Knowledge Publications, 2015.
ISBN 978-1-326-24144-5

Introduction to ISO 14001

A pragmatic approach to environmental responsibility. The logic and concepts that underly the international standard on environmental management.
Orchestrated Knowledge Publications, 2019.
ISBN 979-8-716-72321-4

Health and Safety Without Going Mad

A pragmatic introduction to ISO 45001, the international standard on health and safety. By understanding the purpose, ideas, structure and logic of the standard, you need not do anything that is not reasonable.
Orchestrated Knowledge Publications, 2019.
ISBN 979-8-717-18233-1

Welcome and Thank You

Thank you for picking up my little book. In it, I am looking at helping organisations create a quality culture. By that, I mean an atmosphere within the workplace that encourages and facilitates team members' desire to produce high-quality products and services, even if no one is watching.

Most people really do want to be proud of their work. As a manager or leader, it is your job to remove any obstacles and provide the resources necessary for them always to do their best, and then try for better.

Many books have been published on this topic, and I have read quite a few. Maybe this one is different, maybe not. It does include ideas and experiences I have garnered throughout the years.

If you would like to comment or correct anything, please contact me through my email (see below). All comments, suggestions and critiques are very welcome.

I hope you enjoy reading this and, perhaps, learn something.

Peter Leeson,
OrchestratedKnowledge@gmail.com

Contents

Foreword

My approach to putting these ideas together was long and drawn out. I did not have a revelation; I did not follow a structured creative process, building the concepts from start to finish. On the contrary, my results came mainly from failures, errors, and negative reactions. As I worked in various contexts and roles, I accumulated an ever-growing list of things that did not work and did not produce the desired results.

After eliminating the failing solutions and false answers, I saw what was left. In the following pages, I would like to explain what works once you have removed everything that did not work.

1 Introduction

Quality is a strange thing. People talk about it but never seem able to explain it. Frequently, we only care about Quality when we want to complain when something is not as expected.

We all believe that we want quality, but we are mostly unable to define it or explain it clearly. I want to buy quality, produce quality, sell quality, yet I cannot clearly express what I mean by that word. Typically, people fall back on vague concepts that quality is "good enough to satisfy requirements" or the "absence of defects". Like beauty, we cannot define Quality because both are related to the relationship between the subject and the object. What I see as being Quality is not what you see; in English, we say that "beauty is in the eye of the beholder"; the same is true of Quality.

What makes the quality of a book or a piece of music? A good book (other than respecting basic rules of comprehension, language and grammar) creates a feeling or an emotion that corresponds to my current state of mind or improves it.

In IT, quality is often limited to the "mean time between failures" or "meeting customer requirements". Is that really all there is to it? Is doing just what the customer requested and creating a product that works most of the time sufficient to refer to it as a Quality product? Can I refer to a piece of office equipment as creating a feeling, as

3

music does? Other than irritation at a printer or copier that is not working or a computer that is slow to respond, what other emotions do they create?

How can we ensure we are doing Quality work while doing it? How can we plan for a feeling of pleasure, delight or satisfaction in our customers before showing them the final product?

Organisations rarely consider what level of Quality they want to build into a product or service; they do not consciously define, estimate, plan, design, or construct it. I would go so far as to say that most don't know how to define or quantify it.

The sales and marketing teams are happy to announce and promise it, but they are often unsure what "Quality" means.

> *Quality is most frequently defined by its absence.*

When asked to define Quality, the definition frequently reverts to listing attributes, characteristics or qualities or using quick throw-out meaningless sentences.

1.1 Quality vs qualities

It is reasonably easy to define what qualities are: they are the characteristics of the product or service. If your car is blue, that is a quality. If it does X miles per gallon (or X litres per 100 kilometres), that is a quality. If your software matches the requirements, that is a quality.

But, your *Quality* – with an uppercase Q – is something else altogether.

The Quality of your products and services is that which differentiates you from all the other providers of similar products and services; it is an extra factor that makes yours unique and desirable.

Of course, if you have not met the basic requirements (or qualities), you cannot expect to achieve Quality. Suppose you order a meal in a restaurant and the pasta is cold, the bread stale, or the lettuce wilted. In that case, you cannot expect that the whole meal has sufficient redeeming factors that would still allow you to qualify it as Quality.

1.2   Meaningless sentences

When asked to define Quality, people often tell me that what you deliver corresponds to the requirements. That is not Quality; that is your contractual obligation. You were asked to include a number of features; you were paid to include those features; the least you can do is include those features.

They tell me they don't need a clear definition of its meaning because they have quality people working on designing and building their products[1]. Of course, they cannot define what "quality people" mean and reply with self-referencing loops regarding experience, ability, and "know what they are doing"...

One easy way to recognise the quality people in your organisation is to watch them leave. Your best people will be the first to go when you prove unable to define, develop and deliver Quality that satisfies.

---

[1] I will frequently use the word "product" to refer to both products and services; the alternative quickly becomes tiresome.

1.3   The need to understand

In today's world, we are all confronted with a global marketplace and global competition. Consequently, whatever you propose to sell, I can find somewhere else and probably find it cheaper.

I can probably find a product that corresponds in most characteristics (qualities) to yours but has something that makes it more suitable for my purpose as a customer.

Your competition is probably global, but it is widespread and diverse even in a local market.

Why would I want to work with you rather than with someone else? What is your differentiating factor? What Quality do you offer?

Your competition is not only trying to poach your customers; they include the people trying to poach your employees and potential employees. Are you considered a place where young graduates want to work? Are you seen as a leader, a creative, transformative, and disruptive business focused on the future? Or are you a business producing the same old stuff to the same old customers?

Does your staff want to work for you, or are they only there for the money? What makes you an attractive employer (other than the money)? What are you doing to attract the best graduates and retain your most skilled and competent staff members?

When you produce something new, whether a completely new product or an update, do existing customers automatically trust you to deliver something they will want? Do they buy your products and upgrades without hesitation?

1.4 Defining Quality

You can define Quality any way you want, but you will get into trouble if you do not define it.

- You may decide that you want to be the best in the world, with zero defects.
- You may decide that you want to be the cheapest in the world.
- You may decide that you want to be the first in your market.

You may decide whatever you want as your guiding light, your True North. However, your decision should be clear, and all other aspects need to be subservient to that decision.

Your definition of Quality should consider two options: internal and external. Externally, what will differentiate you from your competition; internally, why are you the best place to work in the business?

2 Emotions

2.1 Does it matter?

If Quality is based on emotions rather than intrinsic factors, does it matter? Surely engineering should not depend on something as intangible as emotions; it should be based on concrete facts and data.

We know emotions are unreliable, and one should not take them seriously when organising commercial transactions. However...

2.2 The Importance of Emotions

Life is a process of continuously interpreting electric signals or impulses received by your brain, locked away inside a dark skull. From birth, we receive a steady flow of signals through our senses. Slowly, we must learn, all by ourselves, without any external help or guidance, to differentiate these signals; we decide what is sound, what is pain, what is pleasure, and what is colour.

We start to interpret these emotions differently. Some give us pleasure, and some stress us. This understanding becomes the guiding light of our physical being. We try to influence the world to increase sensations that give us an emotion we perceive as positive and avoid those we perceive as negative.

Everything becomes an emotion and the focus of all our thoughts and actions.

I will not go further into details on this topic, but I strongly recommend the book "Being You" by Anil Seth[2] if you want to learn more.

Understanding the importance of emotions is critical to understanding the value of Quality. This basis of this relationship was defined by a Roman architect over two thousand years ago, and his teachings still hold.

---

[2] Anil Kumar Seth (born 1972) is a British professor of Cognitive and Computational Neuroscience at the University of Sussex. He has degrees in Natural Sciences (BA/MA, Cambridge, 1994), Knowledge-Based Systems (M.Sc., Sussex, 1996) and Computer Science and Artificial Intelligence (D.Phil./Ph.D., Sussex, 2001). His book Being You explains in easy-to-understand terms the science, facts and principles of consciousness.

3 Vitruvius

The title of this book is "Vitruvian Quality", so I probably need to clarify that somewhat. Let me introduce you to Marcus Vitruvius Pollio, commonly known as Vitruvius. Vitruvius was a Roman author, architect, civil engineer, and military engineer during the 1st century BC.

3-1 - Vitruvius

He was born around 70 or 80 BCE and lived at least until 15 CE.

As an architect, he is known by reputation only. It appears that none of his architectural work survived. The Basilica at Fano is his only known building but seems to have been completely destroyed; no physical trace has been found (yet?).

Architects in the ancient world were not the same as today's architects. Today, architects design nice buildings based on their knowledge of strength, resistance, and other technical or scientific metrics. A Roman architect was expected to be a specialist in many different disciplines, including design, building materials, defence, war equipment, fluids, etc.

Vitruvius is best remembered today for his five-volume oeuvre "De Architectura".

He lays out some basic rules, principles, and more in this multi-volume opus: he describes (among many others) two elements that make him of interest to us:

1. Basics concepts of proportions and
2. The main components of quality.

These two concepts, described by Vitruvius mainly about

3-2 - "De Architectura" by Vitruvius

temples and arenas, remain valid today and form the foundation for this text.

3-3 - - Leon Battista Alberti: Basilica of Sant'Andrea, Mantua

Vitruvius was redis-covered and became an inspiration for the Ital-ian Renais-sance archi-tects and art-ists such as Leon Battista

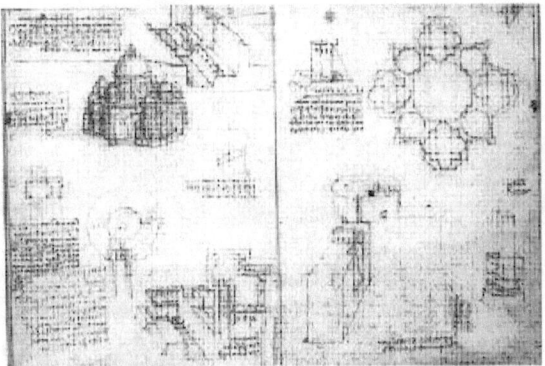

3-5 - Da Vinci Notebook

Alberti (1404–1472), Leonardo da Vinci (1452–1519) and Michel-angelo (1475–1564).

His texts on proportions cover the idea that a man's[3] pro-portions are ideal and should always form the basic pattern repeated throughout a building. Of course, we pri-marily know of his concept of the perfect pro-portions of man through Leo-nardo Da Vin-ci's famous drawing of the

3-4 - 3 2 - MichaelAngelo: St Peter Basilica, Vatican City

"Vitruvian Man" (reproduced on the first page of this

---

[3] Vitruvius did not consider the proportions of a woman to be as per-fect as those of a man – don't blame me.

book).

Those proportions were to be used in design and construction as a "pattern", allowing a form of discreet rhythm throughout the entire project.

> *Proportions create a pattern that is recognisable to humans.*

Christopher Alexander and others refreshed this concept of "Patterns" in the 1970s in two new volumes on architecture and patterns.

The idea of patterns was fascinating. Alexander's books led a group nicknamed "the Gang of Four" to translate the concept into a structure for computer software development.

3-6 - The Timeless Way of Building ISBN 0-19-502402-8
A Pattern Language ISBN 0-19-501919-9

This history of using patterns was reassuring to me as, while it was not my starting point, it showed that the concepts and principles had been successfully used in very different contexts for two thousand years. We should still seriously consider applying them today in various contexts.

In future, we could learn to use patterns and Vitruvian Quality principles to structure management. Until now, it appears they have been limited to engineering practices. It is high time that we move them into other areas.

That's the starting point of Vitruvian Quality: a pattern-based Quality focused template for effective management.

3-7 - Figure 3 8 - ISBN 0-201-63361-2

4 A History of Analysis

4.1 Overview

The Pattern of Management is not a new phenomenon or idea; it emanates naturally from a long series of scientific discoveries and small steps forwards.

The world has moved forward through a continuous series of discoveries and errors. The scientific method claims that theories and hypotheses need to be tested to produce data that proves they are correct or not. Just because your data appears to confirm your hypothesis, it does not mean that a scientific fact: other data and further verifications may show something different. Your data may be a correlation, an exception, a mistake

> *A theory might be true if no one has successfully proven it false.*

While looking through the history of theories and thought processes, one must conclude that most businesses (from both management and engineering standpoints) have remained firmly rooted in the past – including companies claiming to be at the cutting edge of innovation!

In order to understand what I am getting at, let me go through a few of the major scientific concepts that mark our progress.

4.2 Divine Intervention

The oldest form of analysis is the concept of divine intervention. One of the critical characteristics of the human mind is to seek to understand cause and effect. Early on, there was no scientific understanding of ordinary natural phenomena, so humans decided on a reason.

Whatever happens, is caused by some divinity deciding to let or make it happen. If you believe in a good, loving God, you will give thanks for anything good that happens to you; you will trust that something better is in the plan when something unpleasant happens.

Suppose you believe in a more traditional pantheon of gods. In that case, you will accept your fate as related to karma or other divine difference of opinion.

This approach quickly leads to fatalism (don't do anything, wait for the gods to solve the issue) or ineffective solutions: sacrifices to gods rarely produce the desired contextual improvements.

4.3 Analytical Deconstructivism

4.3.1 Overview

Traditionally, in Western cultures, analysis has been done through systematic deconstructivism.

Recently, this has frequently been renamed (or confused with) "system thinking". The basic idea is that a system works because each component satisfies its objective and does its job. Should each component work correctly, the whole system must work correctly, according to the system's design and architecture.

This approach originates from the religious belief that the

designer, the architect, the creator designed every piece to fit perfectly into the grand plan; if you fulfil your role correctly, the planned system will come to fruition. There is no challenge to the ideology of the master plan. System architecture is one of the components in industrial design that needs to be completed as designed.

4.3.2 Impact on Business

When a problem arises in a Western Deconstructionist environment, the first and most natural response is to find out which piece is broken and not doing its job. This attitude rapidly leads to seeking whom to blame for the failure.

In my experience, the majority of organisations in the Western world suffer to some extent from a blame culture. As a consequence, when something goes wrong, a double effort is expended to

a) Hide the mistake by the person who feels most responsible, and
b) Identify who can be held accountable (chastised, punished) for the failure.

The experience invested in these activities could be better used to fix the failure and learn lessons to avoid reoccurrence. This should not come as a surprise, yet many managers remain focused on a destructive, demotivating and counterproductive attitude that places blame above learning.

4.4 Newtonian Mathematics

4.4.1 Overview

Isaac Newton was a peculiar individual. He lived at a turning point in history and was curious about the discoveries – like many others throughout Europe.

The use of tele-
scopes and micro-
scopes changed the
way things were
perceived. The
earth was no longer
the centre of the
Universe: planets
revolved around
the sun. Distant
stars and micro-
scopic beings forced
their way into the
human imagina-
tion. Chemistry
started to appear,

4-1 - Portrait of Sir Isaac Newton by Godfrey Kneller, Public Domain

leading people like Newton to take a more scientific and fact-based approach to age-old alchemy. At the same time, God remained central to daily lives and His laws, as laid out in the Holy Scriptures and explained by the State Church.

Isaac Newton set out the three Laws of Motion[4], the law of Universal Gravitation[5] and Calculus[6], the mathematical

---

[4] 1: A body at rest or uniform motion will continue to be at rest or uniform motion until and unless a net external force acts on it. 2: The acceleration of an object as produced by a net force is directly proportional to the magnitude of the net force, in the same direction as the net force, and inversely proportional to the object's mass. 3: There is an equal and opposite reaction for every action.
[5] Every particle attracts every other particle in the universe with force directly proportional to the product of the masses and inversely proportional to the square of the distance between them.
[6] At the same time, slightly before or after Gottfried Wilhelm Leibniz.

basis for Kepler's laws of motion. He was president of the Royal Society[7], Member of Parliament, Master of the Royal Mint, professor of mathematics at Cambridge University, and a biblical scholar (with a particular interest in Biblical chronology).

Isaac Newton taught us two main things:

- Everything is in movement and transformation,
- Everything can be expressed mathematically.

His fluxional calculus focuses on the mathematical understanding of continual change. It should be taught to change managers in industries everywhere.

4.4.2 Impact on Business

One cannot overstate the impact of Isaac Newton on modern Western thought. We understand the importance of mathematics, statistics, averages, and trends in every industry today.

Unfortunately, this is the level at which most organisations remain. They measure, predict, reward, and manage all activities and people based on numbers (numbers frequently unrelated to anything other than a promise or ambition). While the planets rotate around the solar system with predictable regularity, the same cannot be said about business trends, markets, customer reactions, or staff reliability.

Statistical variation is an essential tool for understanding why things happen or change. The problem is that most managers focus on measuring what is easy to measure (time and money) and ignore what is most critical (moti-

---

[7] Formally, The Royal Society of London for Improving Natural Knowledge.

vation, satisfaction, quality).

4.5 Darwinian Evolution

4.5.1 Overview

Charles Darwin is generally credited with the discovery of the theory of evolution. His theory was a revolution in many areas, not least in the fundamental challenge it posed to Biblical creationism.

The basic concept behind Darwinian theories is that mistakes happen within the reproductive system. Sometimes a DNA link slips and does something different. This mistake would cause a change in a creature's makeup, meaning that the child is not a perfect clone of its parents. Sometimes these "mistakes" create a new strain, ability or aspect that can have one of three possibilities.

1. The change is not noticeable and has no particular impact on the future of the species. It may disappear, remain in place, or become dormant until it encounters another change that activates its potential.
2. The change makes the possessor more attractive to partners or more likely to overcome a particular danger. These changes mean that the possessor is a stronger candidate for the reproduction and continuation of its genetic material. Its descendants will benefit again from this advantage and strengthen it as cross-fertilisation happens throughout the following generations.
3. The change makes the possessor less attractive to partners or more likely to succumb to some danger, predator or disease. This creature is more

likely not to be able to reproduce as prolifically or successfully, therefore killing off the mutation.

Through this reproductive capability, beneficial mutations get reinforced, while detrimental ones die out over time. As someone else said[8], we are all descendants of people who were able to avoid being crushed by falling rocks before reproducing.

4-2 - Charles Darwin

4.5.2   Impact on Business
Many new products, solutions and processes have resulted from accidents and random variations (if not mutations). Perhaps the most famous cases are that of Art Fry using the glue created by his friend Spencer Silver[9] to make the first Post-It note or Percy Spencer discovering the principles of the microwave oven when his chocolate bar melted in his pocket.

---

[8] Sorry, I don't remember where I heard or read this.
[9] Spencer Silver was actually attempting to develop a "super-strong" adhesive when he accidentally created his "solution without a problem"

> *Not every mistake is wrong.*

When one of these proves valuable, it should be adapted and adopted. In many organisations, this variability is not considered acceptable: the focus remains on the policies that "we have always done it this way" or "you must follow the standard process".

4.6 Interoception

4.6.1 Overview

The James-Lange[10] theory of emotions states that we respond first physically; our emotional reaction is in response to physical activity. For instance, if you encounter a wild bear, you do not first feel fear and only decide to run. According to this theory, you see the bear and run; then, the running away is translated emotionally into fear, like you move your hand away from the flame before feeling the pain of the burn. This idea was based mainly on

4-3 - William James

---

[10] Developed by the philosopher John Dewey and named after psychologist William James and physician Carl Lange.

those put together by James and Lange, stating that physiological sensations cause emotions.

Subsequent research pointed to the defects in the theory (including the historical argument that Dewey misrepresented the work of James and Lange and produced a conclusion they would not have recognised). In the early twentieth century, a variation of this theory became more commonly accepted: interoception. This theory postulates that the perception of the body's internal state is reflected in different cerebral regions. A disconnect between the body and organs and the corresponding brain region could cause emotions such as anxiety, depression, and OCD.

Interoception is the basis for understanding allostasis. This suggests that the brain's primary function is to interpret the thousands of signals continuously received and prepare a statistically appropriate response to the emotions, feelings and sensations incurred (or to predict and respond before the emotions occur[11]).

4.6.2 Impact on Business

In most organisations, the management team is considered the brain. The principles of interoception reflect that senior management often reacts to what is coming up from the team members rather than leading them. Senior management teams rarely listen enough to the team's culture[12] to understand and redress the situation before it is too late. As a result, many practices imposed on the workers may prove to be disruptive or slow down the process.

---

[11] This has overlaps with the research by Anil Seth referenced in section 2.2 on emotions (page 9)
[12] I define culture as the way team members behave when they are not being observed or measured.

4.7 Quantum Mechanics

4.7.1 Overview

"Those who are not shocked when they first come across quantum theory cannot possibly have understood it."[13] I will not try to explain what quantum mechanics is or its implication for the world. This text will only give a few key components (at least partially due to my limited understanding).

Werner Heisenberg, Niels Bohr, Paul Dirac and Pascual Jordan discovered and quantified the uncertainty principles of Quantum Physics. They demonstrated that a light-emitting electron is a wave until it is measured when it becomes a particle. Their discoveries opened up the understanding that the future is probabilistic and neither deterministic nor random, as previously thought. It also helps us understand why we can believe two incompatible

4-4 - Niels Bohr

things.

The two most confusing aspects of quantum physics are "superposition" and "entanglement". These are so bizarre that they were rejected for a long time by leading scientists, including Albert Einstein, who claimed regarding these phenomena that "God does not play dice".

In the most simple explanation,

- "superposition" means a quantum can appear to be in two different positions at the same time (e.g. an electron is at two different distances from a nucleus);
- entanglement is the relationship between the observer and the observed, meaning that if you see the electron in one position, that is only real for you at the moment of observation.

Things are not in one state or another but are defined by their probability. Sub-microscopic elements are in a continued state of fluctuation and change. As a direct descendant of Albert Einstein's theory of relativity, quantum mechanics are defined by relationships and probabilities. You may get the impression that quanta are in two incompatible states simultaneously, just as individuals can simultaneously hold two contradictory thoughts.

Another consequence of quantum mechanics is demonstrating how tiny changes, at the quasi-invisible level of the quanta, can have immense consequences and impact. In particular, it was proven that observation and measurement influence the thing being observed.

The three principles of Quantum Mechanics are Granularity, Probability, and Observations.

4.7.2   Impact on Business

Granularity, probability and observations are the three principles of quantum mechanics; indeed, they are the three principles of change.

By *granularity*, we can understand the need to pay attention to what is happening at the smallest level, as that is where we will find the seeds of the culture. Understanding the spontaneous reactions of individuals when facing the apparently most straightforward or evident tasks rapidly reveals the level of support or contempt held towards management and performance.

Probability is the foundation of any sound understanding of business. Risk management and estimating are probability activities typically done by people who do not have the expertise or resources to perform appropriate statistical analyses. Their failings should be expected and accepted.

The value of *observations* has been beautifully demonstrated in the Toyota principle of Gemba[14]. In this approach, management is invited to go down to the factory floor to see the actual problem rather than relying on reported versions.

In traditional, hierarchical organisations, issues are reported through layers of middle management and get transformed through misunderstanding, miscommunication and deliberate misrepresentation. Every level increases the duration necessary to get an answer to a question.

Best go to the source and speak to the front-line people immediately to resolve the issue.

---

[14] Or Genba, 現場

4.8   Systems and Ecosystems

4.8.1   Overview

Bringing all these theories and components together leads us to understand ecosystems better. In traditional system management, there is an understanding that the whole is the sum of the parts. If all the components are working correctly, the entire system should work correctly, according to plans and architecture[15].

The ecosystem turns this somewhat around, pointing out that the individual components depend on the complete system's functioning correctly in ways that might not initially be obvious.

A demonstration of the impact of change on an ecosystem is the reintroduction of wolves into Yellowstone park in the USA. The arrival of carnivorous wolves meant that deer could no longer safely remain static, eating everything that grows. The deers' movement allowed shoots to grow into trees that were not there before. The trees led to the increase in birds, beavers and others. This wildlife and vegetation pro- voked a rerouting of rivers and streams, cooler water, and in- creased fish popula-

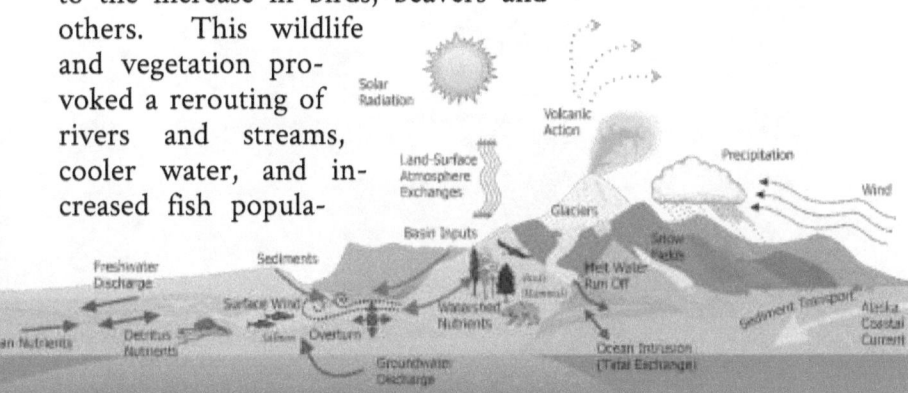

4-5 - Ecosystem Principles

---

[15] See section 4.3 (18)

tions.

No one could reasonably have predicted the results: the presence of fish increases when a small number of carnivores are present.

4.8.2   Impact on Business

An organisation's culture is frequently hidden and results from many unobserved minutiae (quanta). Change at any level can initiate a chain of consequences that must be monitored and understood rapidly to reinforce beneficial traits and curtail detrimental ones as soon as possible.

You cannot force, impose or even significantly change an organisational culture. You can, however, influence it by nudging it in the right direction through minor tweaks to the ecosystem – and that is the main topic of the remainder of this book.

5 The Cultural Ecosystem

5.1 Culture is an ecosystem

An essential lesson from quantum physics is the idea of entanglement: the relationship between the observer and the observed is the reality, and the observed quantum can appear in a different state to a separate observer.

The reality of the observation is also valid within the business world regarding the concept of Quality.

> *Quality is the relationship between a product or service and an observer at a given moment in time.*

What you consider as good quality, I might see as poor quality. The same product can have different reputations in different nations, depending on culture and habits. This duality can be observed in tropical countries as local inhabitants complain of the cold while visitors from Northern Europe or Canada will be sweating in T-shirts.

A similar comparison can be made for individuals: the same man can be a father, son, husband, employee, manager, knowledgeable, ignorant, energetic, or lazy when seen by different people. Rather than considering yourself as a unique being, you are a node in a web of relationships. Your colleagues' perception of you is as much a part of your persona as your left foot or hair, and you do not cease to be you when you get your hair cut.

When you start to consider yourself strictly according to the relationships that you have, with events and with people, you must soon conclude that human society is an ecosystem. Each component, no matter how small, is entirely dependent on the good functioning of the entire system and its continued reliability. This co-dependency was demonstrated in 2020 when we saw how a virus in a Chinese marketplace could completely disrupt the world. Another example is the global economic impact of a local war in Ukraine.

> *We are all defined by our relationships and entirely dependent on the functioning of the global society.*

Naturally, we find the same structure in business between colleagues, management, customer and suppliers.

If we accept that we are defined by our relationships and the perception others have of us, we must examine the corollary. This combination of connections and experience gives each of us a unique view and understanding of the world in which we live.

The network of relationships forms the foundation on which our culture is built. Some relationships are closely linked and influence one another rapidly and easily; others are more distant or even only established through intermediaries. An illustration of how we are all connected can be found in the theory of "six degrees of separation", which claims that any two human beings can be linked through only five others[16].

5.2 The Importance of Culture on Quality

When we start focusing on creating Quality, we must focus on the aspects of culture and leadership. The goal is to create a culture where each individual *wants* to produce high-quality work at every step.

> *The role of a manager is to satisfy the innate desire people have to take pride in the value of their work.*

This requires strong leadership, not just management. Telling people to work hard does not produce results; a culture of mutual support and encouragement to do the right thing will always do the trick.

Let us assume that you have defined what Quality means to you. The next step is to motivate your team members to believe in that vision and believe in you. Changing a culture is not done by telling people how to act: it requires time and hard work from the start, from the top, at every step and every level.

So you need to make sure you start the right way.

---

[16] For a bit of fun, you can test the "Bacon number" of any actor to find out how many roles steps away from Kevin Bacon they are (a step being a film in which they acted with some other actor) at https://oracleofbacon.org. I tested this with the most obscure actor I could find: Grigoriy Aleksandrov, from the 1925 Russian film "Battleship Potemkin", and found he was only 4 degrees of separation away from Kevin Bacon!

5.3 Defining a Culture

When working on defining or changing local culture, we need to be particularly careful about networks and relationships and how we might accidentally break, distort or destroy them. You can achieve destructive results by inserting a single individual into a close-knit community or team[17]. Imagine what you can do when trying to change the culture.

In this book, I will return to the principles of influencing a culture several times, but I need to explain some of the basics.

Every organisation I know boasts of its culture; they all advertise that they are forward-thinking, dynamic, problem-solving, customer-focused, or whatever. Few of them are what they claim.

At the same time, when talking to employees, they always complain about poor communication at some level.

Culture is a pervasive force that inspires and encourages team members to act in a certain way, even if they are not being monitored while they do it. People do what they consider "obvious" or "natural"; they don't understand why you would even question it.

Consider some cultural aspects that you believe to be beneficial within your organisation. How many cultural attitudes on the following list should be in place, and how many are in place?

---

[17] The issue can be easily resolved by ensuring that team members are invited to participate in the interview process and decision making when hiring staff.

- Creativity
- Rigour
- Humour
- Free Thinking
- Challenging and Argumentative
- Rule Breakers
- Rule Followers
- Obedient
- Tolerance
- Right First Time
- Communicating
- Understanding
- Studious
- Fail Fast
- Stick to the plan
- Risk tolerant
- Risk-averse
- Take time to do it correctly
- Deliver early
- Forgiveness
- Economical
- Ethics and social responsibility
- Use proven solutions
- Cutting-edge and innovative
- Report problems early to management
- Focus on solutions, not problems
- Listening
- Generous

Obviously, many of these attitudes are incompatible.

If you want to move a team from a risk-averse culture to a risk-tolerant one, you will expect a long and delicate transformation process. If misapplied, every step could break key beneficial relationships with your cultural network.

When working at changing the way people act, you will need to consider every step very carefully and "nudge" attitudes. To achieve the desired results, your actions will prompt people discreetly to do the right thing, creating slight barriers to doing things that are perceived as negative.

Small actions produce significant effects because we live in a quantum society.

6 The Quantum Society

6.1 Butterfly Effect

The idea behind the quantum society is that we live in a society where everything is connected to the most minor level. The "Butterfly Effect" typically illustrates this idea in chaos theory.

> *A butterfly[18] flapping its wings could cause a storm several weeks later on a different continent.*

E. N. Lorenz[19] used the simile to illustrate non-linear consequences. A more directly observable comparison could be that of a campaigning politician promising something to get elected with no intention (or capability) to implement. Their election could potentially impact people worldwide with a single lie[20].

It is impossible to forecast the long-term impact of any change. However, we can be confident that every change may have consequences at multiple levels, no matter how

---

[18] Apparently, Lorenz originally used a seagull, but was persuaded to change the quote to a butterfly for poetic impact.
[19] Mathematician and meteorologist Edward Norton Lorenz (1917-2008), founder of modern chaos theory.
[20] Compare the promises to the actions related to Brexit as an example of this.

minute it first appears. When trying to change something as profoundly inset as a culture or habit, the change must be carefully processed through small increments and "nudges".

6.2 Nudge

Rather than telling someone to do something or act in a certain way, more subtle approaches can encourage the desired attitude or impede the undesired responses.

Richard Thaler and Cass Sunstein explain this very well in their book "Nudge: Improving decisions about health, wealth and happiness[21]", so I will not go into too much detail here.

Many senior people still believe they can implement a culture in an organisation through slogans, motivational posters of eagles and sportspeople, and mugs displaying warm, fuzzy words. Not only does this approach not work, but it is also frequently destructive, presenting senior management as out of touch and not credible.

Changing the attitude of people needs to be done subtly, delicately. I have worked with one CEO who handed out prizes to team members who reported a rumour that may have distracted them or their colleagues. By doing this, he could be aware of any rumours circulating in the company and address them directly and efficiently. By regularly speaking to the staff and answering questions they had not yet asked, he got them to trust him. He implemented a spirit of openness and mutual trust in which team members were very willing to do more than their strict job de-

---

[21] ISBN 978-0-14-104001-1

scription when needed.

Some simple nudge techniques that can be implemented by management to build trust include:

- Give people more authority to make decisions in their domain, work or expertise;
- Always learn lessons rather than seek whom to blame for failures;
- Listen to concerns and take them seriously: they may appear trivial to you, but they are important to the concerned person.

6.3   Conflict Transformation

Traditionally conflict management and conflict resolution methods have been promoted. These approaches tend to favour attitudes that frustrate at least one of the sides in any conflict. They include deciding to "agree to disagree" or telling one side to "let it go" to appear to eliminate the difference without addressing the real issues. By brushing the problem under the carpet, the conflict is not resolved, and the frustration of at least one of the parties involved increases – seeding the ground for the next conflict.

In "Conflict Transformation", we seek to identify why the conflict arose over time: it is rarely as sudden as observers might believe. Arguments grow over time, from frustrations to resentment to conflict. Rather than focusing on the outcome, we seek to identify the "butterfly" that caused the storm to start.

Once you have identified the underlying cause of conflict, you can start considering what actions to take and turn this into a positive force that allows the organisation to benefit and move forward. Remember that motorcars have been running thanks to controlled explosions inside the engine for most of their history. It may sound as if an explosion in a car's engine must be destructive, but it is what makes the vehicle move.

The same is true of conflicts within your organisation or team: they are the clash of energies that can be transformed into something that helps everyone move up.

I worked for some time with a team member known to have a "difficult" character. I will call him Nicholas. Nicholas tended to get angry and shout at people quite quickly. I realised that he was personally responsible for having implemented many successful processes and infrastructure of the business over its growing years. Every time someone could not do something, they came to ask him to change the security, the controls, the links. Nicholas understood the complexities behind what he was being asked to do and the potential risks of allowing unskilled people to take shortcuts. Explaining this could be challenging, particularly when the requestor did not want to hear any explanations. When asked, he got in the habit of saying "no" immediately. When pushed to explain, he lost his patience and got angry that people did not understand him or his job.

Generally, I have learnt to be more agreeable at work[22]. I get people to explain, ask questions, try to understand and, when I disagree, try to use logic to persuade the other person. Ideally, I ask questions rather than explain, trying to let the person involved talk themselves into an impasse and come to their own conclusion. I had been doing this

---

[22] This is not as simple as it sounds: for most of life I have had a quick temper.

for some time with Nicholas feeling my frustration rise to levels comparable to his. One day, in a discussion with him, I decided to shout back at him when there were just the two of us in a closed office. I interrupted his shouting by shouting louder, told him off, and showed my frustration, anger, and rage.

Something unexpected happened: he calmed down immediately. Over the coming weeks, I discovered I had earned his respect and friendship. He never shouted at me again and never disagreed with me before hearing me out. Things moved on so that whenever someone in the company needed to get Nicholas to do something, they contacted me first and explained the issue; I would then talk to him. We would agree, and either he would do what was requested, or I would explain calmly to the requestor why the request was unreasonable. A few people still tried to go over our heads and demand senior management force him into doing something[23].

Getting senior management to impose decisions on staff is never a good solution, especially when the team members already know that the decision is, at best, risky.

---

[23] This became another issue as, when senior management got involved, Nicholas would come over and complain to me for an hour when that happened, but that's a different problem

7 Organisational Principles

For various historical reasons, organisations have traditionally been organised according to a hierarchy based on medieval kings and barons. The idea is to concentrate authority and decision-making in the hands of a small, centralised group, allowing the "worker" to get on with the task at hand without worrying about strategy or sustainability.

7.1 Mechanistic Management

Not so long ago, in factories, it was often necessary to ensure that the people doing the work were focused on simple repetitive jobs.

Workers assembling Henry Ford's T-Model were not to understand organisational policies or strategies, nor were they to stop work if they knew a better way to do something. Just put the wheel on before the chain moves the car to the guy who screws on the nuts to hold it.

As work moved from factories to offices, the same concept remained in place: the director decides what needs to be done, the manager determines how to do it, the employee does it, and the team leader checks that the employee is working fast enough.

I had one of my first job interviews in the 1970s. This was for a job in an insurance company. Going into the IT department, I saw the rows of people working at parallel, aligned, identical desks. A manager, on a little stage, faced them. I probably went through with the interview, but I knew I could never survive working in that environment.

Even recently (in 2022), when trying to cancel my broadband, a "customer service adviser" on the phone told me she had to inform her manager that a customer was leaving. She left me waiting for nearly ten minutes before coming back to agree to cancel my contract[24] (pending a 30-day notice, which I already knew).

When you are on the front line, facing the customers, you need to be able to make choices and decisions. It would be best if you had the flexibility to respond to questions and issues with as little bureaucracy as possible. Having to escalate every point to your manager is a symptom of subpar customer service and poor management.

The traditional hierarchical approach favours the "divide and conquer" principles. One CIO with whom I worked gave his direct reports contradictory objectives. He believed that if your goals depended on the managers of other departments failing in theirs, you would work harder to get there. The result was a senior team of antagonism and deliberate mutual sabotage. It took me a while, but I got him to change and promote a collaborative approach. He rapidly saw how, together, they achieved a lot more than when competing needlessly.

In recent years, many organisations have concluded that they need to do more than "divide and conquer" and start working more efficiently.

---

[24] No, I will not confirm whether this was with Virgin Media or not.

7.2 Systemic Management

By establishing a clear framework that allows people to make decisions, choices, and even budgets, organisations turned a sclerotic approach into a dynamic ability to respond in real-time to needs.

I will not go into much detail about how such an organisation could work successfully, as described in my previous book,[25] "Orchestrated Knowledge".

The basic concept is to set up a series of "cells" or small groups of colleagues who meet regularly to share and solve their issues and solutions. Cells are based on profession, responsibility and interests. All team members are members of multiple cells, sharing information and knowledge across the organisation.

For instance, a project team will meet daily to settle project-related issues, such as progress, staffing, clarification of requirements, and others. The project managers will meet at least weekly to manage problems related to project management, such as staffing, budgeting, and planning tools. A team member might also be in a cell solving issues or progressing continual improvement, infrastructure, key customer, service delivery, marketing, hiring, conflict transformation, or more.

It is critical, in this approach, to ensure that people making decisions on the front line do so in the knowledge that they are within the organisational framework and objectives. They must know they will not get blamed should their decision not deliver the desired results.

---

[25] "Orchestrated Knowledge", ISBN 9-798718-359237, available from Amazon.

In other words, a decentralised approach to management allows decisions to be made at the lowest level possible. Still, there needs to be a centralised responsibility supporting the delegated authority to do this. There needs to be a head, a structure that coordinates the different branches or arms of the organisation. At the same time, the tentacles and departments have their own decision-making processes and principles.

8 The Octopus Organization

8.1 The Alien Creature

The octopus is an extraordinary animal; it could be extra-terrestrial, considering its uniqueness. It is one of the most intelligent animals on earth. Its obvious intelligence has evolved to be completely different from any other brainy creature.

The octopus can remember, learn, plan and use tools without external training. It has no external protection (e.g., shell, horns) and has been seen to carry large shells, half coconuts or pieces of pottery or glass into which it could hide when travelling to a place where there are few other options. Octopuses[26] have been known to play with balls in aquaria[27] and even playfully splash onlookers. It is possibly the only non-social animal that actively plays.

When hiding, the octopus can change its skin's colour and consistency and disappear entirely in rocks, sand or plants. It

---

[26] The original word is Greek (ὀκτώπους), not Latin. The plural is octopuses or octopodes, but not octopi (which would be a Latin plural.
[27] Yes, "aquarium" is Latin and takes a Latin plural.

reacts to change and mutates its aspect faster than any other known animal. Amazingly, the skin of this colour-blind animal can reproduce the colour of its environment in a fraction of a second.

Having no bones, shell or other hard components, the octopus can squeeze through any hole or tunnel wide enough for its eyeball. It has three hearts, but its most extraordinary feature is its brain.

The octopus's brain is spread out throughout its body. While it has an essential part in its head, approximately one-third of its brain is spread throughout its legs[28].

- When it needs to camouflage itself, the legs can sense the colour and texture and change without communicating with the head.
- Seven of its eight legs feel and taste things to determine whether this can be eaten. If so, they pass the potential food to the eighth leg, which makes the final decision before putting it in the beak to be eaten.
- An octopus can survive without a leg, but the leg can also survive when cut from the animal.

Traditional organisations are set up along the "divide and conquer" principles in which every department or individual has its role, with little or no impact on strategy, policy or customer satisfaction. This is the same principle as our traditional understanding of living creatures. They act like anchovies or sharks.

---

[28] Pedantically speaking, an octopus has legs, not tentacles.

8.2   Anchovies and Sharks

Anchovies are small and quick. They act and react as either individuals or swarms, grouping together to make it difficult to hunt them by stealth. When several thousand anchovies form a swarm, like a murmuration of starlings, they act like a giant entity: changing shape, moving around, creating holes when a predator appears, and closing up again just as fast. The anchovy's thinking happens in its head, which appears to work for it. When in a swarm, they can instinctively react to their neighbour's movement

Sharks are large and generally move slowly[29]. They have survived longer than most species by swimming and eating in a solitary fashion. Rarely do sharks group together.

Some organisations like to be seen as anchovies: they are agile and quick on their feet. They can work with similar organisations when necessary or independently if that is preferable. Of course, they are often easy prey to larger animals. Even when they group, some predators hunt in packs and will catch them.

Some organisations like to be sharks. Sharks have not evolved. They rely on their size and appetite to inspire respect and fear. They roam the business world, eating up any smaller business that looks interesting, killing them off or integrating it into their internal systems, cultures, and structures.

---

[29] At least slower than many fish, I acknowledge that I am generalising here, and some sharks are quite fast

8.3   The Octopus Business

Some organisations work like octopuses. This does not guarantee them superiority or survival, but it increases their chances even when they are small.

The idea is to establish clear and consistent structures, objectives and focal points, then let the people on the frontline make the day-to-day decisions and choices that will improve Quality. Different organisational components, systems, and departments are not in charge of the business and have defined limits and boundaries; they also have the capability and authority to make BAU[30] decisions and investments. They are in charge of their own area.

When a customer asks a question or presents a problem, the person facing the customer should have the option to give a helpful response. A simple example most people have had at some time is the supermarket shelf-stacker. Go to someone working in the supermarket who is busy doing an important job and ask them where you can find Ras El Hanout[31]. Depending on the store, you may find that

- they shrug and say they don't know,
- they go away to ask someone at the back and leave you standing in the wrong aisle for 15 minutes until they return,
- they know what it is,
- they look up on their phone where the product can be found, after which,
    - they might tell you "aisle 12"

---

[30] Business As Usual

[31] It's a spice or seasoning – not to be confused with Ra's al Ghul who is a Batman villain.

- o they go to the aisle with you and help you find it before returning to the work they were doing when you interrupted.

Always allow the customer-facing person to decide whether to interrupt their (vital and urgent) activity and serve the customer. This attitude alone demonstrates the importance given to customer satisfaction, arguably the most crucial factor in quality and organisational growth and survival.

But, if you will empower your staff, you need to give them the power to act accordingly. They need to understand the organisational priorities and have the authority and the skills to act appropriately when faced with unforeseen events.

9 Basics of Quality

As mentioned in the introduction, Quality is the unique differentiating factor of business. While comparable or similar products and services can be found elsewhere, Quality is the defining characteristic of any business and brand. It is separate and distinct from the "qualities" of a product or service, including concepts such as friendliness, portability, ease of use, and others. Quality resides above these and is key to defining the organisation's products, services, and mission statements.

> *People produce quality.*

Processes, standards[32], technology, tools, training, certificates and others are only tooling whose aim is to assist the people in their efforts to produce quality. The same is true of organisational structures. People creating customers' desired products are frequently at the bottom of the pyramid. Yet, they are the ones that make the product or service you are selling; they are the raison d'être of your organisation. Their managers' role is to ensure they have the environment, the context needed to produce quality, including resources, support and protection from unnecessary interruptions.

---

[32] More on standards in chapter 19, "Quality Is Not Standard", Page 153.

9.1   Classic Quality

Vitruvius defined Quality for his buildings as requiring three essential components. I believe these three components of Quality remain valid today in all products and services. If any of them is missing, you may have a product, but you will not have Quality.

1. Firmitas or stability. Your product needs to be reliable in times of trouble, and your walls should not collapse when a gale blows. You should not lose data when there is an unexpected power failure. This aspect is an elementary component of Quality, and if you do not have it, I cannot trust your product or service.

2. Utilitas or usefulness. Your product or service must be useful and respond to a need or desire. Usefulness is usually the area best covered by customer requirements and the main focus of many developments. When disruptive products (like the iPod or Uber) create a demand for something not needed previously, they are still identifying a useful concept and developing the market.

3. Venustas or desirability. Some products focus on desirability over everything else and create something beautiful but not useful. Meanwhile, many others are making things that are useful but not desirable. Getting the balance right between the two is something of an art.

If one of these three is missing, you may have a good product but will not earn your customers' fidelity. Ultimately, you need to create products that will encourage your customers to return to you for more. Your customers want to trust you to provide more of what they want with every new product, upgrade or release.

9.2 Measuring Quality

It is often said that "if you cannot define it, you cannot achieve it and that if you cannot measure it, you cannot define it". It is therefore critical to ensure you have a clear definition of Quality for your organisation. However, few companies manage this first step but continue to advertise the central importance of quality within their strategy.

> *"We don't know what it is, but it is most important."*

Understanding Quality is critical in a competitive world and must be understood in both a qualitative and a quantitative manner. Read that sentence again. Yes, I am saying you need to understand the Quality of Quality and be able to measure it objectively.

What does the Quality of Quality mean? If you have ever used the term "good quality" or "bad quality", you have started to define quality in qualitative terms.

Meeting your customers' expectations is not good quality; it is barely quality: it is the minimum level contractually required. You may believe that having no defects in your product is good quality, but it is not: it is just what is expected (that is why you are required to correct them free of charge).

As mentioned previously, quality is the relationship between a subject (your customer) and an object (your product or service); it is how your customers (and prospects) perceive your products and services.

Quality is not anything intrinsic to the product itself.

Quality is neither objective nor subjective: it is the link between the two. For many years, I have been using the formula Q=P/X to define this concept; it means that **Q**uality is what you **P**roduce divided by your customers' e**X**pectations.

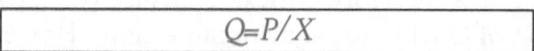

$$Q = P/X$$

I should probably update it and point out that the expectations aspect is much more crucial than previously considered: $Q=P/X^2$ may be more accurate. The speed at which consumers express their pleasure or disappointment on the Internet justifies the increased importance of expectations.

Breaking this down into its component elements, what do we get? I will analyse them from right to left: Expectations, Production and, finally, Quality.

9.3 Quality Expectations

One of the main issues we have today in most industries is the concept of over-selling. Salespeople are usually rewarded based on signing a contract instead of the project's profitability at delivery time. Service providers are paid for time and budget rather than their value. Consequently, they are encouraged to promise more than is realistic, raising expectations regarding the features, schedule, available skills, and more. When all available work hours have been promised, you cannot continue to sell without creating issues. Expectations will be raised unrealistically, and the quality of the work performed will be reduced due to time pressure.

However, the salesforce is not the only one to blame for our failure: it requires communication, understanding and negotiation at the team level. It is rare to find defined expectations: the customer only communicates requirements. There is a big gap between requirements and expectations, which needs to be understood and managed. Articles and theories have promoted the need to talk to the customer and discover the real expectations for decades. In the 1980s, the "spiral software development lifecycle" recommended using prototypes, building a product by adding features and having regular reviews by the customer. Continuous risk management ensured that there was no misinterpretation of expectations.

The spiral or recursive lifecycle is arguably the foundation for the Agile development methodologies through contin-

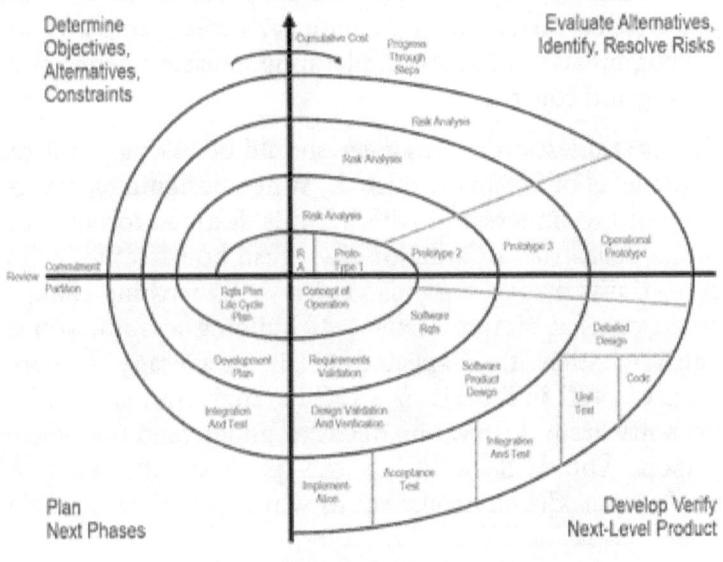

9-1 - The Spiral Lifecycle

uous delivery and change management[33]. The "Scrum" concept integrated another idea from the 1980s: that of "quality circles".

Even the much-maligned "waterfall" lifecycle for software development had a recursive feedback loop and corrective actions frequently ignored by those eager to criticize without research.

The Agile recursive approach is rarely performed as recommended. While the concept is in place, the customer or end-user is not sufficiently involved in the process but is replaced by a "customer representative" whose opinions are guesswork, as (in)valid as anyone else's.

9.4   Producing Quality

Producing Quality requires you to perform engineering practices consistent with an engineer's role: using a valuable combination of analysis, planning, measurement, monitoring and controls.

The first question an engineer should be asking is related to the level of Quality expected. When designing a bridge, you need to understand whether it is destined for an occasional pedestrian or a major city's rush hour traffic, will it carry trains or heavy goods vehicles? Everything changes based on that simple metric. If building a train, you to know whether it is expected to run in average temperatures of -40C in Siberia or +40C in Saudi Arabia. Within the software industry, one needs to understand the type of person who will be using the product, the expected throughput, the environment in which it will run, the de-

---

[33] Although Agile textbooks eliminated the critical concept of recurrent risk analysis.

gree of portability and maintainability required, the potential consequences of failure, and more. In addition, you must understand the resources needed to develop the product: the tools at your disposal, the team's competencies, the level of motivation, the importance of the budget, schedule and quality and more.

When producing Quality, it is not enough for the product "to do what it says". We need to make sure to adapt it to expectations.

Quality engineering should always consider the product's qualities; these qualities should be measurable and demonstrable attributes of the product. Depending on the product type, they may include portability, reliability, flexibility, maintainability and many others.

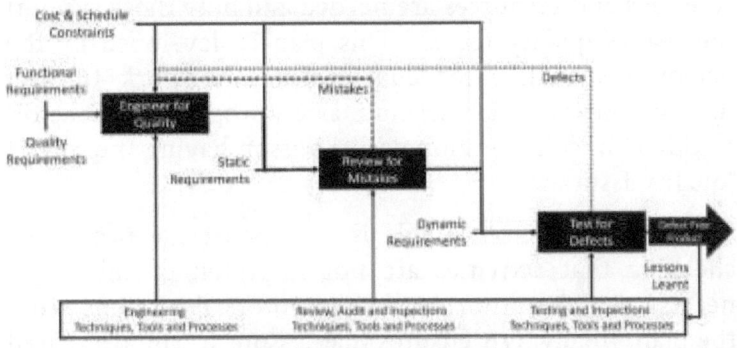

9-2 - Quality Engineering Lifecycle

These qualities can be discussed, quantified and agreed upon with the customer, built into the product, measured and proven to satisfy requirements and potentially expectations; you must take them into account in the engineering phases: designed, developed, embedded into the product, tested and demonstrated.

All people make mistakes; that is a fact of life. The purpose of quality practices, such as quality control and quality assurance, is to remove mistakes early and learn lessons before potential defects[34] demand additional resources to correct the situation.

Engineering quality involves planning, designing and building specific functions and attributes. Everything starts with the plan, which is set up to determine what activities and resources are needed and how these support the team's quality focus. This plan is developed by the person responsible for coordinating the work (project manager, team leader, scrum master, programme director, or other) in collaboration with a person having the role of "quality assurance".

The Quality assurance role is to support the project by checking that activities are not forgotten or missed. If necessary, QA authorises and monitors deviations from the plan; finally, QA ensures that lessons learnt are shared across the organisation. The role of Quality Assurance is to actively assure that team members know what they are supposed to do and are doing it correctly. This

---

[34] A mistake is under the immediate control of the author, it can be easily corrected; a defect has been handed over to someone else for processing, it requires returning to a previous phase and repeating work to be corrected. Once I have finished proof-reading this text and hand it in for publication, all mistakes will become defects.

understanding of QA is very different from quality control which reactively controls the quality of the work already completed through various review and test techniques.

While the qualities are a significant component of the quality of the product, they are not everything.

9.5 Defining Quality

Quality with an uppercase Q is something more than doing what was requested. Producing quality involves impressing your customers with more than they expected; it is the "wow" factor of your products and services.

To produce Quality, in addition to the standard engineering practices, you need to be sure that people know what they are doing and have the means to do it correctly[35].

Quality involves understanding users' perception of the product, including characteristics not covered in the engineering values. Environment, sensory perception, experience, emotions, ethics, language, culture, and others influence the user's perception.

These aspects are rarely understood or managed as efficiently as engineers believe. Engineers tend to trust that most people think as they do, focusing on data and facts. However, "soft" characteristics are frequently more important than the intrinsic engineering quality of the product in the perception by users: colour or language may have a more significant emotional impact than technical skills. Understanding this emphasises the need to understand users' expectations beyond their requirements.

---

[35] Quality Assurance can provide some level of insight into the work being done.

Many engineers don't always understand that not everyone thinks as they do. They might be baffled by a statement such as "I don't like it" when explaining that the new user interface is 87% more user-friendly than previously.

Focusing on Quality means understanding more than the technical aspects of a product: it means understanding the context in which customers will be using it. If you run an airline, this can be relatively easy: your users are all in a confined space that you can furnish and decorate. The problem is much more complicated when creating software to be used in many different places, in offices you have never visited, and on mobile phones in the street. Quality needs more than just engineering skills to be understood and managed; in addition to quantifiable characteristics, we need to build emotion into the product.

Suppose you cannot afford to invest in the sociological and environmental studies necessary to manage this emotional aspect. In that case, you need to be confident that every other characteristic of your product is of the highest technical standard.

Remember that your disappointed customers will be more than happy to share their complaints with the rest of the world.

A bad review may be based on something that appears insignificant to the designer and architect. Still, it is seen as a bad review by the rest of the world. When a product has an average 4-star-rating on a purchasing website, few people bother to find out what stopped some users from giving it five stars. Some bad ratings are due to having a product delivered on the wrong day – that does not impact the quality of the product.

Basics of Quality

10 Quantum Interference

Over the past century, scientists have slowly come to grips with the sub-microscopic world of quantum mechanics. Management has remained firmly trusting in the concept of "scientific management", as defined in 1877 by Frederick Taylor. I have already covered this in some detail earlier on[36].

10.1 Taylor and Scientific Management

Just a few words of context, this is not important for now.

One main idea behind scientific management[37] is the focus on financial efficiency. The approach was further refined and expanded upon, using a variety of names, including logistics, process management, business process reengineering, lean manufacturing, six sigma and others.

Through time and motion studies, Taylor determined the optimal way of doing any specific task to increase productivity. He also identified that staff were not motivated to do more than necessary and recommended that remunerations should be linked to output. In themselves, these do not seem to be controversial concepts. It may have gone too far when Henry Ford applied this by creating the pro-

---

[36] See 4.7 Quantum Mechanics, page 24.
[37] Taylor originally named this "shop management" or "process management".

duction line and reducing humans to machine components.

One element of Taylor's work was the observation of the worker. By measuring the worker under varying conditions, he determined that the fact that you show an interest in their well-being was critical to their productivity. The story goes that he increased the lighting in a factory and saw production go up for a while, then went back; he decreased the lighting and saw production go up again. He concluded that management needed to show an active interest in the workers, which was sufficient. I read somewhere[38] that they changed the lighting on Sundays when the factory was empty. They then compared the performance of the (rested and refreshed) Monday workers to that of the preceding Saturday, at the end of a long, 6-day week of 10-hour shifts.

10.2 Quantum Observation

Taylor's idea that you needed to show an interest in the workers was critical. But perhaps he did not fully understand the physical impact of observation.

In his brilliant book "Helgoland"[39], Carlo Rovelli writes about his first encounter with quantum observation. I will try to restate his experience here briefly[40].

---

[38] Sorry, I don't remember where I read this.
[39] Helgoland by Carlo Rovelli, ISBN 978-0-241-45469-5, original publication 2020 Adelphi Edizioni SpA. I have borrowed the graphics from his book, but recommend you read Rovelli's account to get the full details.
[40] Feel free to jump to section 10.3 if you want to skip the quantum magic and go directly to "The Impact of Observation" on management.

A stream of photons was generated by a weak laser and split in two through a prism: half the photons went down the left path, the other half down the right path. They were reunited before being split again into two streams: one up and the other down.

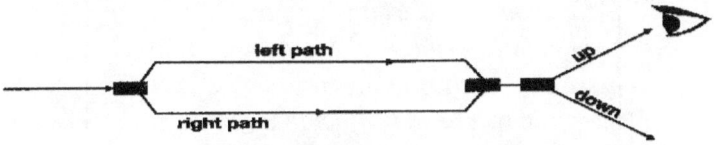

A beam of photons is separated into two by a prism, reunited and then divided again.

If either the left or right stream was interrupted, the photons would split the second time as expected, with half following the "up" channel and half following the "down" channel.

But when both were allowed to flow freely, all the photons followed the "down" channel.

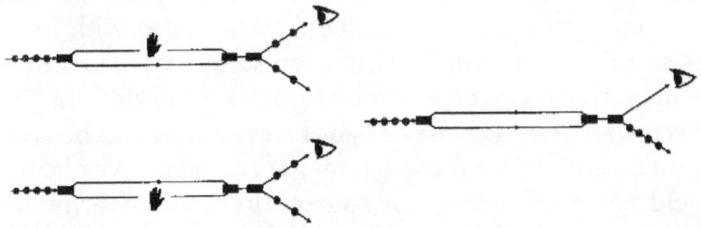

Nobody knows why this happens.

If this was not weird enough, wait until you hear what Rovelli did next.

When Rovelli measured (or observed) one of the two paths, the photons reacted as if they were being blocked!

> *"It seems that you need only to observe for what is happening to change! Note the absurdity: if I don't look for where the photon passes, it always finishes below. But if I look at where it passes, it can end up above. The astonishing thing is that a photon can end up above even if I haven't seen it. That is to say, the photon changes trajectory due to the fact that I am waiting for it at the gate, on the side where it hasn't passed. Even if I haven't actually seen it!"[41]*

10.3   The Impact of Observation

Taylor was right, and quantum physics is right: observing and measuring have an impact on behaviour – including that of people you are not observing.

The "Oxycontin" opioid scandal of the 1990s in the USA hit some states more than others. The states with lower levels of opioid overdoses and prescriptions had implemented the requirement for triplicate prescriptions[42] as doctors realised that they might be measured and behaved more carefully than those whom government investigators could not easily trace. Of course, the state governments

---

[41] Helgoland by Carlo Rovelli translation ©2021 Erica Segre and Simon Carnell.
[42] Every prescription for a pain killer (or drug that is not listed on the official list), one copy to be kept by the prescribing doctor for two years, one to be kept by the delivering pharmacist for two years, and the third carbon copy sent to the state government. Prescription pads were made by the state, every prescription traceable back to the doctor.

did not have the resources to check every prescription. Just the idea that someone might be observing was sufficient.

When measuring a team's performance, attitude or productivity, you will influence the behaviour of that team. You will also seriously influence that of other teams that know someone is being measured. There are various reasons for this, the most obvious being

- Management is taking this seriously and investing in making things happen;
- We might be the next team to be measured; we had better be prepared.

Of course, the resulting attitude created by metrics is not always positive. The focus may move to satisfying management's expectations in terms of data rather than the customer's expectations in terms of Quality. We have all heard of organisations who spend their remaining budget in December out of fear that, if they don't, it will be cut the following year. This attitude creates extraordinary amounts of waste to please bureaucrats behind their spreadsheets.

As you focus on satisfying your sales quota, you start pressuring customers and R&D staff. You reduce costs, make promises that cannot be held, and push for delivering products that are not yet fully finished and tested.

If you want to change things, you must implement some measurements and controls, but you must do it carefully and for the right reasons.

11 Making it Happen

Producing Quality cannot be done through a series of policies, key performance indicators and processes. Quality must be produced by people who want to deliver it, supported by controls that identify system failures, rather than blame the people concerned.

Of course, goodwill is insufficient; we need to implement some level of control. It doesn't matter that you are embarrassed about your mistake if it is your fault and has led to problems for customers, colleagues or management. Mistakes happen, and controls are there to discover, identify and remove them as soon as possible.

11.1 Changing the Organization

Changing the organisation is an activity that must occur at every level. Some aspects may be relatively simple to implement; others are a lot less so. We must focus primarily on the organisational culture to change an organisation. We need to focus on the human attitude to doing things, which means institutionalising activities that seek to change how people react to events within the organisation.

To change the culture, we need to work on the individuals' mindset, seeking to get them to accept the change both intellectually and emotionally, acting accordingly both instinctively and after reflection. The challenge we face is to provide the people involved with sufficient evidence and support to change four aspects.

1. Acceptance: they need to understand why something is necessary. It may be unpleasant, but all the evidence shows that this is required, and things would be worse without it ("I accept that I need to pay more attention to my health").
2. Ability: they need the skills and expertise to do what is required. Providing the ability involves ensuring they have the resources, time, tools, knowledge, and training to do what is needed ("I have a gym near my home and can afford the fees").
3. Aspiration: they must want to do it and actively desire the results. Their desire is such that they eagerly perform according to the established principles ("I want the body of an underwear model").
4. Attitude: the most challenging aspect to change is to get team members to do what is necessary spontaneously, without thinking. They consider the desired attitude natural or normal. They wonder about (or challenge) colleagues who do not act accordingly ("I think I'll just sit on the couch and watch another episode...").

11.2   The Challenge of Change

Several techniques must be deployed to change staff members' culture or attitudes. These include methods such as emphatic interviews, education rather than training, reward and recognition, continuous active listening, and others.

If people are not doing what they are supposed to be doing, there is a reason. Together, we can find the cause and help them move on with the necessary support and encouragement.

For quality to be produced, the people doing the work need the right motivation.

11.2.1 Acceptance

Accepting the need to do something is the rational acknowledgement, on reflection, that this is the right thing to do.

Acceptance does not mean that one does the right thing.

Acceptance	Ability	Rational
Aspiration	Attitude	Responsive
Reflective	Reactive	

Before anything can be done, the people involved must accept that change and improvement should or must happen. They must believe in the idea of change, the need for a new way of doing things, and a different future.

Some people may accept the need for change through information, education, training and seeing the data. However, many will need more than this. Confirmation bias is only one reason why people will reject the facts that don't confirm what their instinct or their faith suggests. You will need to get emotional[43] acceptance before this can be considered complete.

Consequently, you probably need to consider different and complementary ways to persuade people and get them to believe and accept the need for change.

11.2.2 Ability

Ability is about having a reasonable possibility to react correctly and rapidly.

Ability does not mean that one does the right thing.

Providing the ability to do the right thing combines many things. It includes ensuring the people concerned have the knowledge and skills needed to do the work correctly; they also need the tools, technology, time, and budget.

A significant investment is required to ensure that when it is needed, the people concerned have everything they need to do what must be done rapidly. Unfortunately, many organisations only react too late. They don't see the value of training or providing backup resources until it is too late.

During a period of slow business, like a recession, an intelligent leader will see the inactive staff as an opportunity to provide education and training, develop new products or services, and prepare for the future. The majority of organisations focus on saving money and reducing staff; as a result, when business picks up again, they find they don't have the resources needed to respond.

A crucial part of providing the ability is ensuring a risk management (and mitigation) approach to identify the ur-

---

[43] See chapter 2 on Emotions (page 9) for more on this.

gency that could lead to needing additional resources, skills or knowledge.

11.2.3 Aspiration

The sincere desire to do something is critical to success.

You want it, understand the cost, appreciate the benefits, and are willing to invest the time, money, and effort required to do what it takes.

Investing is not enough: you will fail if you do not *really* want it.

A classic example is the number of people who stop smoking unsuccessfully. If you stop smoking because you feel you should, you will probably not quit for long. The most challenging step is not to stop smoking; it is to decide that you actually want to. Once the genuine desire is there, you are willing to put up with a few months of struggling, and you will understand that you can't have "just one" a few weeks later.

Having the aspiration to change or progress is perhaps the most powerful motivator. However, it will only generate more frustration without acceptance of the need or the ability to act accordingly. Providing the aspiration on its own is the fastest way to alienate your best team members.

11.2.4 Attitude

Finally, change management's most challenging aspect is changing the attitude.

Attitude is a psychological construct that combines mental and emotional aspects typical to each individual. When we start talking about the attitude at an organisation level, the level of complexity becomes enormous.

Your attitude is closely linked to your instinct. It is your rapid reaction to something without thought or analysis.

Changing the attitude, like changing the culture, is a complex[44] situation, meaning you cannot define it or make it happen directly. Still, you should be able to identify the constraints that facilitate, encourage or impede attitudes. By carefully nudging those constraints, you start getting the possibility to shape attitudes to something more constructive.

Once your team members have accepted the need and have the ability to act, if they have the aspiration to see the outcomes, your most significant issue is not to stand in the way of the attitude.

You want to encourage team members to respect basic rules and policies while at the same time recommending potential improvements to the way things are being done.

The most important aspect of attitude change is to ensure that the key objectives are well defined and staff is *educated* in understanding why things are required or critical. Of course, once this has been established, it is indispensable that senior management leads by example and never undermines principles by acting differently to requirements.

Changing the attitude requires more leadership than management. Changing the culture is an exercise in complexity thinking.

---

[44] The Cynefin framework (see next chapter) defines "complex" has as a context where there are enabling constraints that facilitate or impede the probability of a result – but are not sufficient to guarantee the outcome. By contrast, "complicated" situations have governing constraints that can be identified after the fact. "Obvious" situations have well-defined constraints, and "chaotic" ones have no constraints.

12 Complexity Thinking

12.1 Cynefin

Dave Snowden and Cognitive Edge developed the Cynefin framework[45] to help organisations identify and resolve issues by understanding their level of complexity and potential for resolution.

The framework essentially defines five categories for problems which are listed below.

- *Obvious*: we know the constraints, they are fixed, and we can rapidly resolve the issue as we have done many times before. If a product fails for a known reason, customer service responds accordingly.

12-1 - The Cynefin Framework

- *Complicated*: some governing constraints work together

---

[45] https://www.cognitive-edge.com

to create the problem. Some research and understanding will allow us to respond appropriately. The use of experts is here to help build a plan on how to resolve the issues at hand. We have lost a significant portion of our market share and are unsure why; our internal expert can analyse the problem.

- *Complex*: there are a series of enabling constraints, meaning that they did not provoke the incident, but we can determine retroactively that if X had not happened, Y would not have occurred. The best approach, in this case, may be to experiment, evaluate and repeat as often as necessary to move the issue from complex to complicated. A foreign war, a storm in the Indian Ocean, a strike in Finland and the short-term policies of a populist government have caused a breakdown of our supply chain.

- *Chaotic*: things happen, nothing we could have done or foreseen. It just happened that way. Call it fate or destiny, karma or God's will. These issues typically require rapid action to respond, followed by more detailed research. Our CTO has been hit by lightning while playing golf.

- A fifth area, called "*disorder*", is for the issues that have not (yet) been classified in one of the four main areas when you cannot figure out where you are or what needs to happen. One could argue that all issues start here, but you must get them out of this purgatory as rapidly as possible.

- Additional liminal areas are included because few things are simple enough to fit into a single box.

An essential lesson in the framework is that, while you can

move issues around the framework from one state to a neighbouring one, you will never be able to cross from "chaotic" to "obvious". Complicated problems, if repeated, can become obvious the next time around. Complex issues allow you to discover new practices that enable you to learn and move them into complicated ones. Chaotic problems can ultimately be resolved and move into the complex quadrant. One of the most common mistakes I have witnessed is the tendency to use a simple (obvious) solution to a complex problem, thereby moving it into the chaotic zone.

Mismanaged obvious problems can rapidly become chaotic. They then need to be restructured to allow them to move through complex and complicated before they can be brought back to where they belong. An example of this that I have witnessed many times is in the software industry. An organisation claims to sell a standard product tailored to your specific needs. Unfortunately, the salespeople tend to demonstrate the latest product version, as it was tailored for their most recent customer. The customer now expects the particular tailored options to be in the standard and add their own bespoke requests. In very little time, the engineers find they need to maintain, often under warranty, a different standard for every customer. Upgrades to operating systems are nightmares as fifty various "standard" products with incompatible features are on the market, expecting service simultaneously.

This section is a very brief and simplistic overview of the Cynefin framework, and I strongly recommend that you take the time to learn more about it as it is handy, particularly when trying to explain complexity to managers and team members.

12.2 Complexity

The key state I want to cover here is the issue of complexity. In my opinion, most problems are created by trying to implement simple solutions to complex questions without proper escape routes from the potential consequences. Populist politicians frequently demonstrate this as they get elected on quick-fix slogans to fix endemic problems (e.g. blame foreigners).

When facing a management problem, in other words, when dealing with people, you can assume that the problem is always at least complex – few people are satisfied by being complicated.

> *People issues are at least complex, and*
> *some people are chaotic.*

There is no easy way out or clear guidelines, manuals or constraints. Of course, you might identify that a person's ill-advised comment caused the current level of disrespect within the organisation. However, that is not the only reason: that comment only made public, strengthened, enabled or confirmed an existing situation.

In a complex situation, you cannot plan, from the start, the route to follow to reach the desired destination: you have to work systematically, step by step, to ensure you are going in the right direction. When I was young, I did orienteering, particularly with the scouts. In this discipline, you are dropped off somewhere with a map and a compass and told to make your way to a given point. There is no direct road. There is no public transport. There is not even clear visibility. The approach is:

1. Identify your exact position on the map – this needs to be a high-definition, detailed map (GPS did not exist in those days).
2. Identify the precise direction in which you wish to travel based on your position and the location of the end-point.
3. Use the compass to check the direction and find some marker you can reach (a tree, rock, tower, house).
4. Make your way to the marker and start again from step 1.

This approach is the same as how we make our way out of complex issues: step by step. Hopefully, every step is more or less in the right direction and does not have counter-effects (you may come to a wall you cannot cross). The goal is to recalibrate, measure, aim and take another step until you approach the place you want to be.

When trying to solve a complex issue, the traditional approach of planning the shortest way will typically fail due to its optimistic outlook.

Complexity thinking allows for continuous path correction until you achieve the result.

Similarly, when moving towards the culture change you want in the organisation, you need to define the endpoint and slowly work on how to get there, step by step. That is what I am going to talk about in the following three chapters.

13 Changing the Culture

Every team leader and every manager desire an organisation where everyone *wants* to give their maximum, do their best always to satisfy the stakeholders and deliver high quality.

Few manage to implement a culture of quality that motivates team members to go the extra mile.

13.1 Defining the Outcome

13.1.1 The Culture Issue

When dealing with people, we always have prejudices and desires that may be realistic; we have expectations and preferences, whether we are aware of them or not.

For instance, there is a proliferation of research papers available about the smells to which we are attracted or not. More to the point here, we are attracted or repulsed by people based on attitudes and actions.

Someone caught out lying for self-gain is generally judged as someone with whom we might not want to be associated[46]. While many organisations take pride in advertising their culture, the advertised culture is not the one staff members experience. Management promotes a culture of openness and professionalism but is in the habit of seeking

---

[46] Although many politicians appear to navigate this issue…

who to blame when something does not go as expected.

They continue to hope that, by talking about it, team members will believe them and change their attitudes.

13.1.2 Defining the Culture

If you want to establish a culture in an organisation, you need to think about it carefully and consider the potential ramifications.

- A culture of honesty may encourage staff to tell demanding customers to stop asking for things; it will also authorise team members to point out your personal failings and weaknesses.
- A culture in which people do as they are told and focus on their job may lead to a heavy bureaucracy in which stagnation is preferable to improvement.

The list goes on. No perfect culture will allow all the amazing things you read about in management magazines and hear about in TED talks.

> *Define what you stand for before you*
> *define the culture you want to see in your*
> *organisation.*

So, the first challenge is to define what is truly important to you as an organisation[47].

It would be best to decide your priorities before determining what you actually really want. Also, and just as necessary, is determining how your cultural objectives may be used against your true desires.

---

[47] See section 5.3 on Defining a Culture (page 34) for a list of incompatible attitudes and cultures.

Measurement is a way to limit interest to a given area at the expense of everything else. If you plan on supporting your culture transformation with progress metrics, be aware that the results will rapidly be misused if these metrics are used to establish progress, a leadership board, benefits or punishments.

Measurement has been the religious obsession of management for over a century. While useful in crucial areas, it is also one of the foundations of failure, as attention is focused on getting the numbers at the expense of the entire ecosystem.

13.1.3 The Job to be Done

Defining the job to be done should be a preliminary requirement for any activity, but rarely is. When you purchase a product or service, it is to fulfil a job, which might not always be the one that is expected.

You might purchase a book to use up your time while waiting or travelling, to learn something new, to feel the excitement of suspense, to dream of better people, places or times... None of these objectives is the primary concern of the printer and possibly were not even in the mind of the publisher, editor or author[48]. However, if you understand that your readers are people who want to dream of beautiful love stories, you will focus on creating happy-ending romances with relatable characters.

The same is valid here. We all want the same impossible outcome – just like your customers wish for perfection, immediately, for free. You want your team members to work hard, be happy inside and outside of work, not bring

---

[48] Some authors appear to write specifically for airport and train station kiosks.

their problems to work, not get sick, work 80-hour weeks without tiring or getting burn-out, and gratefully accept the lowest possible salary. You want the most intelligent people to recommend better ways of working and changing the rules. At the same time, the majority continue to work as they are told without questioning or arguing. You want them to continue working with the equipment in place and keep up to date with new equipment, techniques and tools on the market – without requiring you to pay for their training or going to conferences and tradeshows during working hours.

Once you come down to earth again, we can start considering what you really want them to do.

- What work ethics would you rather see being practised within your team?
- How much do you trust your team members to do the right thing? How good are you at hiring competent people?
- Do you believe that the workplace "happiness index" has a significant positive impact on customer satisfaction?
- Do you emphasise continual improvement or respect for the "way we do things"?
- Is technology change significant for your business?
- How much should team members understand customer issues?
- What is more critical: cheap supplies or suppliers who work as partners?
- Do my team members understand my goals? Do they agree with them? How do I know?
- Do I understand my manager/shareholder/owner's goals? Do I agree with them? How do I know?
- Are my goals aligned with my stakeholders' goals?

There are many more questions you should ask yourself before deciding on the traits you genuinely want to encourage or discourage. Also, you must, naturally, be ready to abide by the rules you impose.

You are the Culture!

Culture is how people behave when no one is watching or monitoring them. It is pervasive in the organisation and affects all interactions at every level. More importantly, culture is often inherited from the leader.

In 2020, this was particularly visible in the UK. After imposing a complete lock-down due to the Covid-19 pandemic, the staff working closely with the British Prime Minister felt the rules should not apply to them and organised parties that finally led to Boris Johnson's downfall.

Once you have decided what you would like the final result to look like, you need to understand your starting point objectively.

13.2   Discover the Starting Point

If culture is how people behave when they are not watched or monitored, it becomes challenging to determine what needs changing. How can you observe, measure, or understand how people behave when they are not being observed or measured?

13.2.1 Anonymous and Confidential

In my experience, this is best established by an external, unbiased person. It involves getting people throughout the organisation to open up and speak freely about what they like and don't like, what supports them in their work and what appears to be an impediment.

13-1 - Team Issues and Satisfaction

You must guarantee anonymity and accept that there are no right or wrong answers.

Personally, when I have performed this work as an independent advisor, private discussions with staff members at every level have been conducted to discuss their work, motivation, and frustrations. I want to understand what they consider a high-quality job in their work and what would motivate them to perform more effectively. The independence and confidentiality of the approach allow participants to complain about management, colleagues, customers, requirements and expectations, tools, processes, support, guidance, coaching, or whatever they want to discuss. It is a free conversation.

Another approach is to use triangulated questions. These questions require more preparation and can limit the scope that can be covered. The idea behind triangulated questions is to allow the respondent to balance out two or three key factors to answer a question.

In illustration 13-2 - Triangulation, the person concerned has asked a question and received a

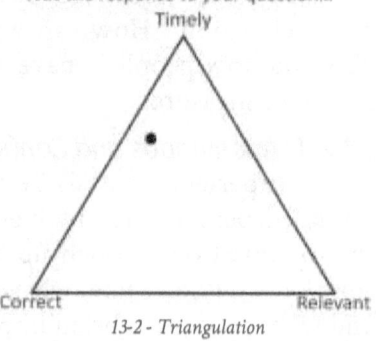

13-2 - Triangulation

response. To judge its value, they determine whether the response was given fast enough, if it was relevant to the question (or context) and/or answered the question correctly.

Suppose they place their mark in a corner. In that case, it could signify something significantly wrong (e.g., the answer was timely but neither correct nor relevant). Rarely will the mark be placed precisely in the centre of the triangle (or line if only two options are given). This approach allows respondents to provide opinions that are not perceived as negative or incriminating.

Other approaches can help satisfy issues more or less rapidly through various exercises.

One such exercise I do is ask a group of people questions they are unlikely to answer accurately[49]. They discuss in small groups, estimate and give their confidence level in the result. The interesting part

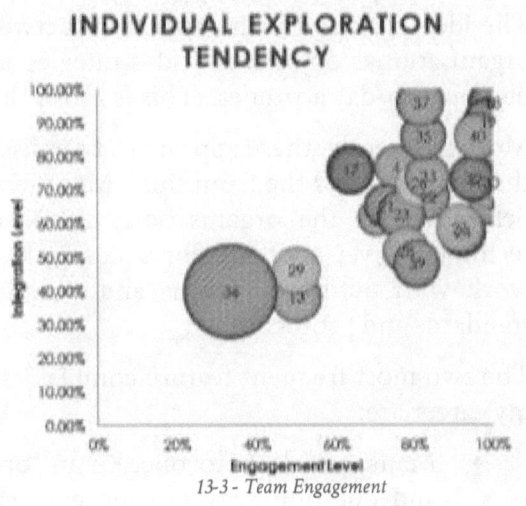

INDIVIDUAL EXPLORATION TENDENCY

13-3 - Team Engagement

---

[49] E.g. What is the height of the Great Pyramid of Giza? When was the Magna Cara signed in England?

comes afterwards, when asked to fill out a short question-naire about the process. Now, they are asked whether they were personally involved in the response, if they personal-ly agreed with it, and more. This exercise produces much information regarding the respect for different people's opinions and skills at every level. This approach allows me to rapidly create a diagram highlighting the individuals' level of integration, engagement and skills (see illustration 13-3 - Team Engagement).

The basic idea of all these approaches is to independently, objectively and anonymously collect indicators of the or-ganisational culture and satisfaction levels.

13.2.2 Accepting Diversity
The ideal situation is the alignment between the top-level organisational objectives and strategies and team mem-bers' day-to-day attitudes. This is rarely the case.

More frequently, there appears to be a disconnect between the hierarchy and the front line. Management might pub-licly advertise the organisations at the cutting edge of technology, yet staff members complain that they must work with outdated systems and comply with rigorous standards and protocols.

The two most frequent feature complaints I have found in my career are:

- Managers claim to operate an "open-door policy" and question why no one ever comes into their office to ask a question or raise an issue;
- Communication. It seems everyone complains about communication: too much, too little, too late, too frequent, irrelevant.

Rarely does the management team concerned conclude

this is due to their own shortcomings. This diversity of opinions and preferences can be drowned in the continual blame game: it is always someone else's fault, isn't it?

Once everyone has expressed their opinions, desires, beliefs and frustrations, a significant piece of work is to go through this and find what is critical. We need to differentiate between causes and consequences and decide what is someone's personal problem versus what is a potentially systemic issue that one person only raised.

Experience is necessary to judge, prioritise and start building an approach to get from where we are to where we want to be.

13.3 Design the Evolution

As described in section 12.2, Complexity (page 80), changing an organisation's culture is a complex problem that needs to be resolved carefully and systematically.

Having identified the starting point (section 13.2) and the desired outcome (section 13.1), we now need to plan carefully how to get from here to there.

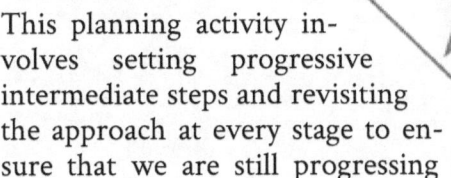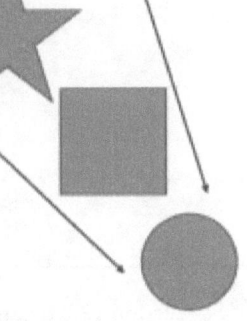

This planning activity involves setting progressive intermediate steps and revisiting the approach at every stage to ensure that we are still progressing in the right direction[50].

Dramatic changes imposed by management will always fail. You cannot dictate culture change through policies and posters, but you need to understand the components that are progressively influencing the culture, encouraging team members to do the right thing, and discouraging them from doing the wrong one.

Many organisations believe this can be done through a process of bonuses and reprimands, using regular performance reviews to hammer in the message. However, a pecuniary gain is a very short-term motivation. Most people are happy to receive a raise but realise, within a couple of months, they have spent the extra money and forgotten the reward – only a massive bonus might have a longer-term effect. Also, a raise in salary quickly leads to the expectation of another for the recipient and their team-mates doing a similar job.

However, changing the culture is possible if you are willing to make the necessary effort and understand the risks involved.

---

[50] See section 12.2 (page 78) for more on this approach.

14 Risk[51] Management

Changing contains risk.

Changing an organisation at any level presents significant risks.

Changing something as profound as an organisational culture presents enormous risks.

However, there are no endeavours without risks. To manage change and improve Quality, you need to establish a Culture of Quality – and that means understanding the risks and being willing to take appropriate actions to mitigate them.

Very rarely can risks be avoided entirely; however, they can be mitigated through several approaches, including:

- Reduce the probability of the risk occurring,
- Reduce the impact of the risk when it occurs, or
- Have a "plan B" ready should the risk become an issue.

---

[51] There are two camps in the risk professionals: those who believe that risks always have detrimental results, while opportunities have beneficial results, and those who talk about positive and negative risks. Personally, I fall in the camp of calling opportunities risks as well, but in this chapter, I will only be speaking of detrimental risks.

14.1 Identifying Risks

Identifying risks is an everyday activity we all perform every day. Most risk identification activities are things we have learnt young and remain with us throughout life. Daily risk identification activities include looking before crossing a street, holding on to the bannister, wearing your seatbelt, brushing your teeth, etc.

Within the workplace, team members continuously identify risks but frequently do not report them. They do this for any of many reasons:

- They assume someone already knows and is doing something about it;
- They believe that this is outside their remit and ignore it;
- They have been burnt for "bringing bad news" to management.

It is vital to encourage everyone to look continuously, every day, all the time, for what might be going wrong and documenting it. Management should be looking for risks and welcoming any that are reported to them

> *You can only do something about it if you know about it.*

People should be nervous if they have identified a risk and not reported it; likewise, they should never be anxious about reporting it. Of course, some things reported are not risks. This might be because the person identifying it does not have all the elements. Perhaps the risk is already being managed, but it is better to have a known risk reported several times than encounter an issue because someone did not speak up.

Team members must feel involved, concerned, and affected by the organisation and its future. They worry about things going wrong, whether minor problems create an annoyance for the staff or significant incidents that could lead to serious legal or financial consequences.

Now, I do not expect every team member to be able to judge whether a risk is big or small or determine how to mitigate it. Still, I do expect them to communicate all risks they believe may exist in a retrievable manner[52].

When working with a team, I typically hand out a pack of "sticky notes[53]" and recommend that they write down any risk or impediment as soon as they think of it. Write it down, review it later and decide whether to report it, deal with it, or realise you didn't have the facts.

Like most people, I frequently suddenly think of something that appears obvious. I trust myself to remember it, only to vaguely remember when the time comes that there was something I was supposed to remember, but what? We continuously think of risks and things that need to be done in our daily lives. We wake up in the middle of the night thinking of risks, concerns and issues. Few of us take notes, and we soon forget what we promised ourselves to do.

Most issues and problems are foreseeable; nothing is worse (in my opinion) than hearing someone say, "*I knew months ago that this would happen. Why didn't they do something?*"

---

[52] By retrievable, I typically mean in writing, but this can be in many different forms – what matters is that the people concerned (including potential auditors) can retrieve the reported risk in the future.
[53] Post-It® Registered Trademark with 3M

If you thought it might be a risk, *you* should have done something; at the very least, you should have communicated it to someone with the necessary knowledge, competence, experience or authority. *"They"* do not know everything and might never have seen the risk.

Please note the turn of phrase I used: *"this might be a risk".* Perhaps it is a risk, and perhaps it isn't; what is certain is that we will never know if you don't do anything about it.

It is strongly recommended to monitor the number of issues that were never identified as risks. Why were they not documented? At what point could they have been identified? What were the precursor signals? And most important: how can we make sure we identify these in future?

One way of getting started in risk identification is using the history available: what were the issues on our previous, comparable projects? Making a list[54] of risks is an approach that can help many individuals give it the correct level of thought.

14.2 Assessing Risks

Risks need to be quantified so that they can be prioritised. A detailed list of every potential risk that could be identified by someone will rapidly contain several hundred risks. You cannot manage, let alone mitigate them all.

When prioritising risks, three factors need to be considered:

---

[54] Organise your list to create a taxonomy of everything that could ever go wrong.

1. The probability that this risk will grow into an issue;
2. The impact the risk will have should it turn into an issue;
3. The time frame in which the risk is most likely to become an issue.

In a perfect world, you would want to state that there is a 47% probability that X will happen on 12th January, costing us an extra $45683. In the real world, it is a lot more complicated and imprecise. However, it would be best if you attempted to get realistic estimates.

14.2.1 Probability

Possibly the easiest step in quantifying risks is determining the probability.

This estimate should not be made harder than it is. You probably can rapidly say that it is likely, probable or possible that something will occur. As you progress, you may identify that things will be "almost certain" or "highly unlikely".

As you progress, it becomes helpful to put numbers on these words to make them more concrete. Starting simple, we can place a 20%, 50% or 80%[55] probably on risks. Then, as they accumulate, you might need intermediate values as "this is more likely than X but less than Y". The more risks you consider, the better you will be at identifying probability.

A simple exercise to increase your skills in estimating probabilities is to remember to track them throughout

---

[55] Never 0% or 100%. If the probability is 0%, it is not a risk but an impossibility; if the probably is 100%, it is not a risk but an issue.

their life cycle. After a while, you should be able to prove that you were estimating correctly: 20% of the risks you estimated at 20% should become issues. If more than that become issues, you are under-estimating; if fewer, you are over-estimating. And, over time, you can refine your estimates.

Of course, you may make random guesses initially, but that is acceptable if you analyse and refine your approach over time. Estimating is a skill; the more you do it, the better you get.

Probability	Uncertainty	Rank
>80%	This frequently happens in our industry	5
61%-80%	This has happened at least every (project duration)	4
41%-60%	This has happened at least every (project duration)*2	3
21%-40%	This has happened	2
<21%	I am not aware of this having happened	1

14-1 - Example probabilities based on history

Your knowledge of your industry can further refine the probability. Look back over the past few years and decide, in your industry, what is the track record. Based on your historical knowledge, you can determine the probability of a similar incident reoccurring in the considered timeframe.

14.2.2 Impact

The impact of a risk can be felt in many ways. Sometimes it is obvious, but, more often, it is not. What is the potential impact of a dissatisfied customer in the age of social media? Is it better to deliver a finished product late or an incomplete product on time?

When reporting the cost of a risk, it is best to be able to give an impact in measurable terms rather than a generic statement that it might be a "big" risk. The question is how to decide the probability the customer changes their mind and updates the requirements costs $5247.00. There is a way to quantify even the most abstract approach, but it needs to be applied with care.

Remember, metrics and measurements focus attention on a single aspect of a problem and make other elements less critical. In the long-standing debate about climate change, key decisions have to be made by politicians, who are more focused on the next election rather than on future generations. Consequently, they focus on making commitments for after they are out of office (please the environmentalists) but avoid short-term actions that may upset financiers, taxpayers, the oil industry or their sponsors.

When you decide on a quantification approach, you need to consider why you are doing it and what might be the best metric to achieve results. This means translating the risk into the financial cost if your management focuses primarily on profitability or social costs if that is their key declared focus.

When calculating the impact, you may need to work in two streams, one based on data and the other based on "gut feeling[56]".

Some risks are easy to quantify.

- The only impact is that your product may be released two months late. You can calculate the cost of keeping the development team together two months longer and any external financial

---

[56] Gut feeling is the result of your subconscious accumulation of experience and history. It is frequently more reliable than expected.

impact (loss of sales, factory delays, customer penalties).

- A team member will leave: speak to HR about the cost of hiring someone new, including advertising, interviews, training them up, and impact on the productivity of the new person's mentor.
- The probability that someone will be taken ill during your project is statistically the same as how many people were sick in past years.

Others are a lot more difficult and will require some imagination as well as legwork:

- If the office moves to the other side of town, how many would leave rather than do the additional commute[57]?
- How will customer satisfaction be impacted if the product is considered just "good enough"? How many customers will we lose? How long before the competition can make something better based on our product?
- The probability that a key individual is taken ill at a critical moment is difficult to estimate. The likelihood is low, but the impact may be enormous.

I usually recommend estimating as many risks as possible and then determining the impact of others in a relationship with those you know.

---

[57] I ran into this with a client. The rumour was they would move, and the rumour-mill was working hard at it. We calculated that they had lost nearly 35% of their productivity by people talking about what if, whether, should, but... Once senior management understood the problem, they clarified the situation for all employees and things could go back to normal.

14.2.3 Prioritising Risks

An easy way to prioritise risks is to create a grid in which they are spaced out with probability on one axis and impact on the other.

This approach allows you to place rapidly (instinctively) the risks you cannot quantify around those you can. Once you have a few risks you can quantify, you can estimate those risks around them (for which you have decided this is more likely than X but has less impact than Y.

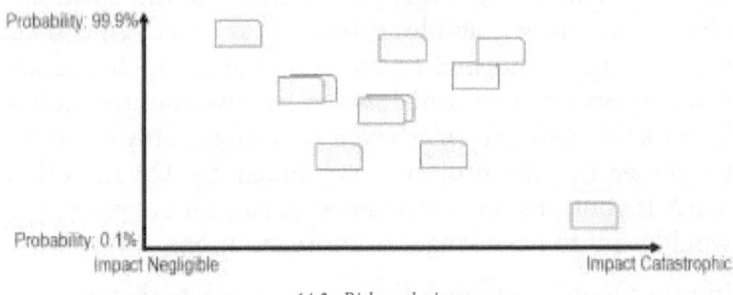

14-2 - Risk analysis

Based on your abilities, you can determine which risks you want to mitigate by selecting two boundaries to separate those that are sufficiently important to work on immediately from those you will monitor and those with which you believe can live.

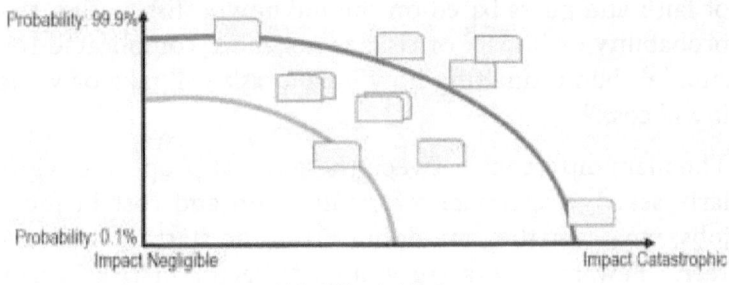

14-3 - Risk prioritisation

This brings us to the next point: when is a risk likely to turn into an issue?

When prioritising risks to determine which ones must be managed and which ignored (for now), you must consider the time frame: a medium risk for next week might be significantly more important than a big one for next year.

Again, this estimating activity need not be particularly complex. Risk timeframes can be easily classified into imminent (next week), short-term (next month), medium-term (next quarter) and long-term (next year). Of course, these categories depend on the job's duration. If you are working on a project scheduled to last two months, defining risks as medium-term when they might only occur after the end of the project is not practical. On the other hand, if your project is scheduled to run for six years, you would want to have longer or more durations.

In other words, establish time-frame buckets that are reasonable for you and your team, but establish, document, communicate and agree on them.

14.2.4 Estimating Techniques

Estimating is never easy.

You always come to a point when you need to take a leap of faith and guess based on the unknown. Estimating the probability or impact of risks is not more complicated (or simple) than estimating how long a task will take or what it will cost.

The main difference between these is that people are regularly asked to estimate effort, duration and cost in most jobs, whatever they are doing, from the start of their career. Few managers are willing to factor in risks when reviewing or accepting estimates. They are more likely to argue that a task is taking too long or costing too much than ask whether risks have been considered.

> *When reviewing an estimate, always ask if this is really enough[58].*

When you start estimating something new, don't worry too much about it: you will get it wrong, except by a miracle. However, by tracking actual costs and relating them to the original estimate, you quickly learn to estimate costs and values more accurately.

Percentages and probabilities are slightly more difficult to monitor as you must watch how many risks never became issues and why. However, this is possible. On average, 20% of all the risks you estimated at 20% should become issues; 50% of all those you estimated at 50% should become issues.

After a while, you will improve your estimating skills through this kind of monitoring.

14.3 Mitigating Risks

Having defined the main risks that need to be managed immediately, you now need to decide what you can do about them. There is a limited number of things that can be done about risks: you need to reduce the probability or the impact, which can be done by one of several approaches.

---

[58] Customer satisfaction is increased by under-promising and over-delivering; but commercial pressures tend to push businesses to over-promise and under-deliver. Imagine how nice it would be if you could regularly receive your products earlier than expected, with a refund or discount on the budgeted amount for time saved...

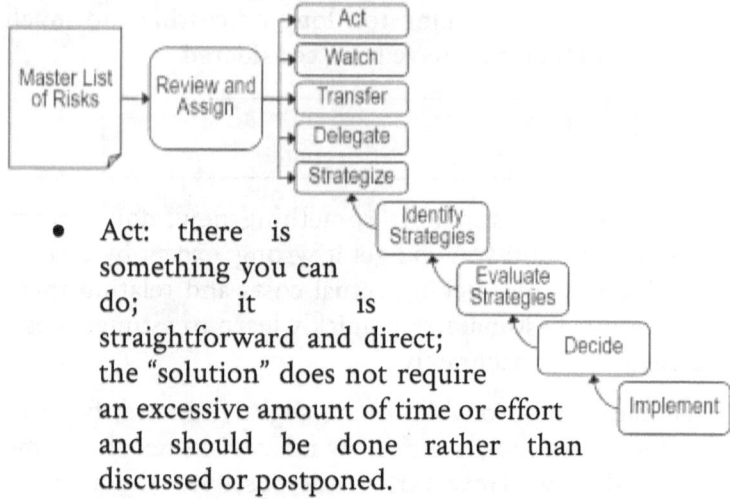

- Act: there is something you can do; it is straightforward and direct; the "solution" does not require an excessive amount of time or effort and should be done rather than discussed or postponed.
- Watch: the risk is not critical in the short term, and we should keep an eye on it; once it has grown (either the probability or the impact has increased), we will decide what to do. Meanwhile, we monitor the risk on a monthly or weekly basis.
- Transfer: the risk needs to be managed, but, realistically, there is little you can do about it. Transfer this risk to someone else: put penalties on your suppliers if they don't deliver on time, buy an insurance policy in case your assets catch fire.
- Delegate: the risk is internal to your organisation but outside your scope, remit, authority or responsibility; this is a risk that you will delegate up or down: your management needs to decide how to respond, or you can pass it on to someone in your team who is better placed than you are about the approach to take.
- Strategise: some risks are more complex and need careful consideration of the best approach. For these, you should compare various strategies.

14.4   Mitigation Strategies

There can be many ways to reduce risk; sometimes, it is worth considering the cost and value of each one.

First, identify different potential strategies which may have a positive impact. I recommend that you identify at least two possible solutions that might reduce the impact or probability so that you have a point of comparison.

Once you have identified a few general ideas, you can compare these approaches: quantify them and determine the amount of effort and cost involved in implementing the solution. Remember to also factor in the remaining risk, as it is very rare indeed that you can eliminate a risk.

Your risk leverage is based on risk exposure before and after mitigation and the cost of mitigation.

$$RiskLeverage = \frac{RiskExposure_{Before} - RiskExposure_{After}}{RiskResolutionCost}$$

Your risk exposure here, ideally, would be the multiplication of the potential financial impact and the probability of the risk turning into an issue.

Suppose you can calculate your risk correctly as a 75% probability of a €10000 overrun. Say that, after a mitigation effort costing €4500, your probability is reduced to 33%. It becomes relatively straightforward to calculate the risk leverage[59]. The strategy with the highest leverage is the best approach.

If a risk cannot be translated into quantifiable values, it probably indicates that it has not been adequately understood. Learning to quantify the imponderables is a lesson

---

[59] ([10000*.75]-[10000*.33])/4500 = 0.93

that needs to be learnt[60].

14.5 Using Risks

Once you have understood the risks of not changing and those of the changes, you can compare these two and determine the better approach.

If you decide to change how things are being done to reduce your overall risk level, you can start working on the constraints that limit your potential.

---

[60] I recommend for this a number of books by Tom Gilb or Douglas Hubbard. Depending on your particular focus, each one of these two authors has excellent material on measuring the seemingly abstract.

15 Cultural Constraints

Many of the statements and recommendations in this text refer to an implicit need to improve organisational culture. Some will tell you that you cannot change the culture, that it grows and happens, and that you need to learn to work and act within the confines of the culture.

While it is certainly not easy to change a culture, it can be done. It needs to be done carefully, consistently and consciously.

A community's culture comes from the sum of all the experiences, habits and knowledge of the people involved.

Personal beliefs and attitudes grow from physical aspects (DNA and heredity), upbringing, education, and more.

Nature + Nurture

Every book, film, trip, experience you have ever had, every melody to which you listened, all these work together to make you a unique individual with instincts, habits, biases and knowledge that are not shared by anyone else.

Bringing these together into a community creates a wealth of knowledge that forms the group's wisdom[61] or culture.

---

[61] Wisdom is defined, in my mind, as the sum of knowledge and experiences that allows you to react correctly and rapidly to unexpected

A community's culture is the sum of the relationships and interactions between individuals, between individuals and their environment, and within an individual[62]. Culture is a very complex issue and cannot be easily changed because it depends on many constraints that enable the system to work. Culture forms an ecosystem in which every component plays a critical role in maintaining the balance, and every component is dependent on the balance of the whole system.

When seeking to establish a quality-focused culture, you must make an effort to define what needs to be changed and why. The more significant step then comes from identifying the constraints that enable the culture to remain and which can be influenced to promote changed attitudes.

This step is the requirements and needs phase of your culture design.

Once these constraints are identified, there is a need to implement a "constraint management" system to ensure that they are tweaked as needed.

15.1   Understanding Constraints

Previously, I briefly referenced the Cynefin Framework (see chapter 12 on Complexity Thinking, page 77). This framework divides problems into categories based on constraints. Constraints, here, are the things and events that enable, facilitate, or provoke results. It is essential to un-

---

circumstances and events.
[62] Communication within an individual includes the communication between neurons or between the brain and muscles, between past experiences and current context.

derstand the concept of constraints before we can proceed.

Constraints are events that have occurred (or occur on a repeatable basis) that limit the options of what might happen next.

You can generally recognise constraints as you consider an issue or risk and conclude that "this only happened because three months ago that choice was made".

Complex
probe-sense-respond
Enabling constraints
Emergent Practice

Complicated
sense-analyse-respond
Governing constraints
Good Practice

Chaotic
act-sense-respond
no effective constraint
Novel Practice

Obvious
sense-categorise-respond
Fixed constraints
Best Practice

Generally, there are two categories of constraints that are of interest to us:

- Restrictive constraints due to which the possibilities of what happens next are limited ("if I hadn't broken my leg falling off my bicycle when I was six years old, I could have been a long-distance runner");
- Enabling constraints that allow something to become possible ("if Iceland's Laki volcano hadn't disrupted the weather and caused droughts and famines, the French revolution would not have occurred").

Constraints are typically links in a chain of events that often lead to unpredicted results.

When trying to change the course of events (or the culture of an organisation), we need to consider the constraints that can be identified. We can then determine if we can influence those constraints. Finally, we focus on how. Exploiting constraints is a delicate mission that needs to proceed with delicate nudges and continuous awareness of the potential risks and consequences. Every nudge presents a combination of opportunity and danger.

15.2   Theory of Constraints[63]

Nudging constraints to generate a change requires a few key steps:

15.2.1 Identify the constraints

As mentioned previously, you need to understand what is facilitating the status quo and what might encourage a change of attitudes.

These characteristics might include things as varied as national or regional attitudes, management not acting according to their own rules, agreeing to customer requests without understanding the impact on the team required to deliver, and more.

Identifying the constraints requires, in many cases, objectively and independently analysing, listening, examining and accepting.

For example, I will consider an organisation where most staff members are doing their 9-to-5, respecting the rules, but are never available to perform additional work when needed. So, let's consider potential constraints that may lead to this:

- Overtime is taken for granted;

---

[63] See Eliyahu M Goldratt's book "the Theory of Constraints" (ISBN: 0-88427-166-8) for more on this topic.

- Management is perceived as more focused on respecting the rules than understanding the needs and concerns of staff[64];
- There is no respect or appreciation of the effort made;
- Promotions are limited mainly to a small group of management's close friends and "yes-men";
- There are no real options for career progression unless you are in the "inner circle".

These are common issues that affect staff morale, and I have encountered them frequently. There are many more, and you must conduct a listening exercise inside your organisation to determine the significant influencing factors.

15.2.2 Decide how to exploit the constraints
Accepting that the constraints establish limits to what can be done, the next step is to decide how to best evolve within those constraints.

Once you have determined *and accepted* the constraints, the next step is to decide what can be done. Don't seek to solve all your issues simultaneously. Your effort will fail if you try to do too much; you may succeed if you focus on the primary constraint.

Let's take one of the elements mentioned above: "Management is perceived as more focused on respecting the rules than understanding the needs and concerns of staff".

Maybe management is too focused on rules and regulations, maybe not; what matters here is that team members

---

[64] I mean that management is more focused on making others respect rules, standards and policies. Unfortunately, many managers do not respect their own rules.

believe them to be so. How can we remove that perception? How can management appear more friendly?

Some ideas:

- All management team members have lunch at least twice a week with their team members. They don't do this in the executive restaurant, but with the team members where they usually are: the canteen, hot-dog vendor, cheap pub down the road. One CIO I convinced[65] to have lunch in the canteen told me afterwards that he was amazed how junior employees "treated [him] like a colleague" instead of the boss.
- Implement a structure that allows staff members to work remotely, perhaps from home, on a regular basis.
- Establish a procedure to resolve "personal emergencies" rapidly without impacting pay or reviews. If a child is sick and needs to be picked up, this should be possible in a few seconds, warning someone about it and going – without asking permission or filling out forms.
- Communicate clearly that the company objectives are to complete the activities and do a good job. They are not just to be present in the office at any given time or for a set number of hours.
- Never ask for overtime unless there are extraordinary circumstances that require it. Even then, seek out volunteers.

---

[65] It took me months of harassment to get him to go to the company canteen; when he finally went, he had no idea how things worked and I had to pay for his lunch.

- Reward effort discreetly in ways that go beyond the legally required[66].
- Trust your team members so that they may feel they can trust you. If you don't trust them, you will lose their trust.

> *Overtime is always a sign of bad management*

15.2.3 Subordinate everything else to the above decision

Whatever the constraints, there must be a way to limit or reduce their impact.

You made a decision, chosen a solution, an approach. You have prioritised the management of constraints. This new approach must be a golden rule, to be obeyed publicly and visibly, at every level, from the senior manager to the local team facilitator.

As soon as senior management allows an exception to the decision, it loses all credibility among staff.

15.2.4 Elevate the constraints

To elevate the constraint, we reduce its limiting impact or increase its enabling impact to meet the desired results.

---

[66] An organisation with which I was working delivered a software development product on time, and the team was widely rewarded (with an all-expenses paid trip to a resort), this was widely publicised, and an internal newsletter published their praises for having done what they had agreed to do. Meanwhile, the maintenance team was working extraordinary hours, seven days a week, trying to correct the errors and failings in the delivered software and keep the client from suing – this was not rewarded or even acknowledged. The development team had been led by a friend of the CEO. A significant number of maintenance team members left the company in the following months.

As we elevate the constraint, we slowly move towards the point when it breaks, achieving the desired effect.

Stay with it, do not give up. You might not see results for days, weeks, months or longer, but the constraint will remain unchanged for years if you do not stay with it.

In large organisations, the regular turnover of senior managers can jeopardise the effort made. What can you implement that will not allow your successor in six months to break everything and start something contrary to what you have achieved? And are you willing to implement a change that might only reach fruition after you have left?

15.2.5 Go back to step 1
If you have broken a constraint, don't expect your problems to be solved; go back to step 1[67] and identify the next major constraint.

15.3 Nudging[68]

Telling people to do something rarely works efficiently for long. Publishing a policy on a company intranet never works. Having meetings to announce new slogans is generally a waste of time.

Constraints need to be delicately nudged. You need to make it just a little easier to remember and do the right thing and a little more challenging to forget or ignore. See chapter 6 (page 37) for more on nudging.

Nudging people is an art and a science. It requires a care-

---

[67] paragraph 15.2.1.
[68] See *"Nudge"* by Richard Thaler and Cass Sunstein (ISBN 978-0-141-04001-1)

ful understanding of potential motivation[69] (because people are not motivated by money for long). A typical example of this can be found in the example given in Thaler
and Sunstein's book "Nudge" regarding tax compliance:

> "In the context of tax compliance, a real-world
> experiment conducted by officials in Minnesota
> produced big changes in behavior," of taxpayers were
> given four kinds of intormation. Some were told that
> their taxes went to various good works, including
> education, police protection, and fire protection. Others
> were threatened with intormation about the risks of
> punishment for noncompliance. Others were given
> information about how they might get help if they were
> confused or uncertain about how to fill out their tax
> forms. Still others were just told that more than 90
> percent of Minnesotans Groups already complied, in
> full, with their obligations under the tax law.

> "Only one of these interventions had a significant effect
> on tax compliance, and it was the last. Apparently some
> taxpayers are more likely to violate the law because of a
> misperception - plausibly based on the availability of
> media or other accounts of cheaters that the level of
> compliance is pretty low. When informed that the
> actual compliance level is high, they become less likely
> to cheat. It follows that either desirable or undesirable
> behavior can be increased, at least to some extent, by
> drawing public attention to what others are doing. (Note
> to political parties: If you would like to increase turnout,
> please do not lament the large numbers of people who
> fail to vote.)"

(Extract of "*Nudge*" by Richard Thaler and Cass Sunstein, Penguin
publishing, page 72)

In the next section, I will discuss Vitruvian Quality and
some basics for changing the organisation. The approach
goes beyond the concepts of nudge and focuses on coher-

---

[69] See "Drive: The Surprising Truth About What Motivates Us" by
Daniel Pink (ISBN 978-1-84767-769-3)

ent and consistent communication through every means.

16 Vitruvian Quality Components

The VQ method seeks to ensure a common, consistent and coherent approach throughout the company based on the concept of quality. The idea is that by implementing these practices rigorously, we can start to elevate the constraints that may be limiting your effectiveness.

The term "Vitruvian" relates to the principles laid out by

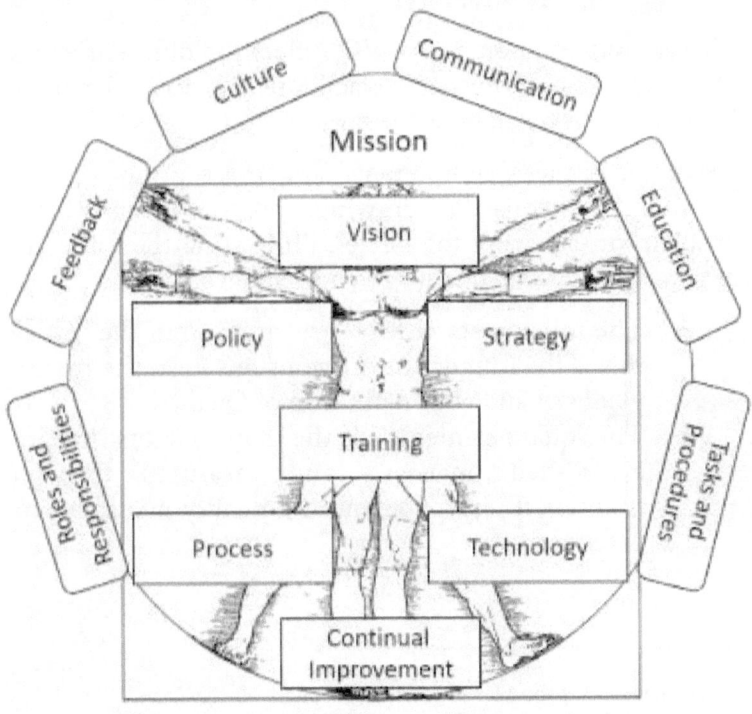

16-1 - Vitruvian Quality

Vitruvian Quality

Vitruvius[70]:

1. Proportions of your building, product, or service should always reflect the proportions of man. Going monumental so that man cannot relate will lead to failure.
2. Patterns ensure that the proportions of the most prominent elements are reflected in the smallest. Consequently, the human size is recognised, even when the whole is the hugest element.
3. The product, service, or building needs to reflect the three key components of Quality:
   a. Stability,
   b. Usefulness, and
   c. Desirability.

The various components of VQ reflect the different levels of communication needed to facilitate a structured culture focused on delivering Quality.

I structured these components into three groups corresponding to Leonardo's drawing and to the unsolvable problem of "squaring the circle", illustrating the difficulty of getting corporate quality at a human level:

- The mission statement is separate from the rest as this is the foundation for your business, the reason you exist and your definition of Quality.
- The square elements are the "hard" factors that are established, managed and measured through traditional improvement and quality management practices.

---

[70] See chapter 3, page 11 and section 9.1, page 54.

- The circle elements are the "soft" components that influence the people doing the work and are traditionally more challenging to manage.

Together, we have the full Vitruvian Man, as represented by DaVinci, containing the Vitruvian Quality list of principles.

16.1 The Mission

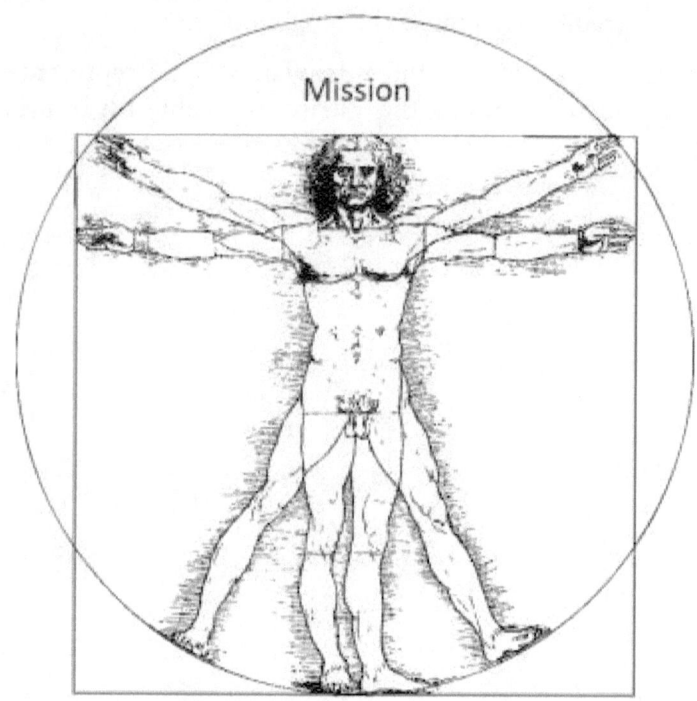

The start of any business needs to focus on the mission. What are you trying to achieve? What are you planning on doing to change the world? Why do you believe you have something to offer that is better than the competition or something that does not currently exist on the market?

> *Your mission statement is the keystone of your business*

The mission statement is not just an advertising slogan. It is the company's keystone, where you set your critical differentiating factor in stone. You don't want to be the same business as your competitors; you want to make a difference in the world and inspire trust. If you are just in the business of making money (and are not a bank), you will not inspire your staff or customers.

Suppose your mission is to provide "honest, reliable, efficient" products and services. In that case, that *always* needs to remain the true North of your organisation. Whatever you do should focus on honesty, reliability and efficiency. In the future, you may be tempted to overcharge a particularly annoying customer or claim a tax rebate for a personal expense as a business one. If you give in to these impulses, you will have ruined your mission and lost the trust of your staff, customers, and market.

Sooner or later, the truth always comes out.

16.2 The Square

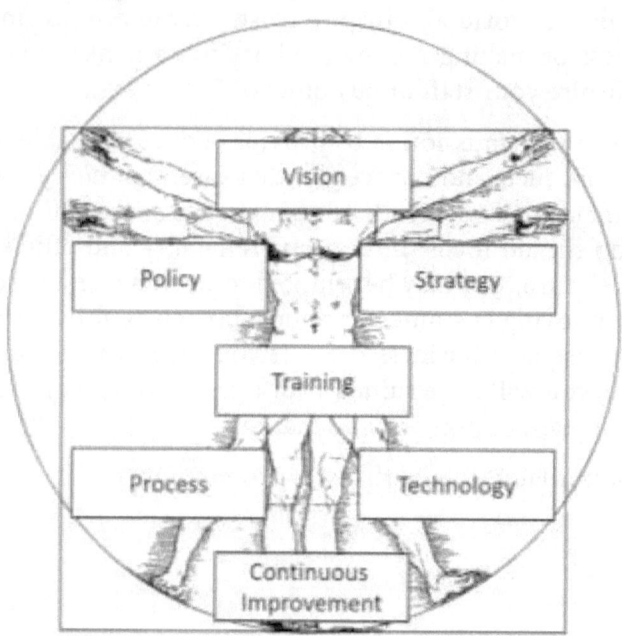

16.2.1 Vision

I have frequently been surprised by the lack of vision of senior executives. As a former auditor and consultant, I always started my missions by asking the CEO (or the highest-ranking person responsible for the area under consideration) what their vision was. Why would a potential customer want to come to them rather than to their competition in two, five or ten years?

Most senior executives thought the world would continue as it is. They didn't need to think of the future; they just managed day-to-day problems as they arose. Some were truly disheartening and saw the future strictly in terms of higher profit levels. One told me they would attract new customers *"because we are so good at fire-fighting"*. The only way you become good at firefighting is by having many fires; for a commercial product business, that appears to be the worst situation possible[71].

> *Where there is no vision, the people*
> *perish.* (Proverbs 29:18)

The vision is essential. The world is a rapidly changing and shrinking place. If you have no competition at the moment, expect one very soon, and they will be better than you at something. You must be ready for change, motivate teams and prospects, and plan how you will tackle future challenges.

Every organisation needs two visions. The traditional marketing vision statement, communicated on websites and information leaflets, is focused outwards and speaks of what an excellent company, product or service this is.

The second vision statement is an internal one. It is a clear and concise statement focused on the members of staff and motivating team members as to the values of the organisation and the culture you hope to inspire internally. This vision needs to be stimulating for the employees, contractors and subcontractors. It enables them to vali-

---

[71] I used to work for a software company that frequently sold products that did not live up to expectations or commitments. At the time, I was usually the one that needed to go solve the issues all over Europe. The CEO once introduced me to a customer as the "Red Adair of the business". Paul "Red" Adair was known at the time as the top firefighter in the world, regularly being called in to extinguish fires in petrol drilling wells, like after Sadam Hussein set fire to all the wells in Kuwait in 1991. I thought at the time that this was flattering for me, but as a prospect I would not want a company that is used to setting fires in the customers' sites.

date the activities and communications coming from management as being in line and supportive of the vision statement.

As with the senior executive question referenced above, I have frequently asked staff members: "why would you want to work here in two, five or ten years, knowing you could earn more money elsewhere." The response shows the true motivation of employees. This understanding should be used to determine your vision.

Your vision statement is the practical side of your mission statement. While the mission statement may be grandiose and even utopic, the vision is the reality check. It defines the status of things on the way to achieving the ultimate goal.

To establish your vision, consider your mission statement and define what would be different if you achieved it. Your mission statement may be high-flying and unrealistic, but what practical difference would it make? Suppose your mission statement is that you want to reduce the difficulties for poor people to access the benefits of the internet. Your vision statement might reference the internet providing businesses, improved wireless communication across non-profitable areas, or developing cheap data-processing tools.

Your vision shows the desired real impact of your mission statement in the short, medium or long term.

16.2.2 Policies
Some things will be required to move towards your mission and achieve your vision for the future.

These may include ethical, environmental and social aspects that cannot be bypassed. Formalising these requirements is the objective of your policies. Your policies will establish your attitude and understanding of what you consider non-negotiable. Policies are meant to be equivalent to the "constitutional law" of your organisation. They describe the things you will not compromise, the actions and attitudes that are not negotiable. The policies are laid out, explained, and clear and must be respected by everyone, including the CEO.

The company policies identify the culture of the company. A policy should be in place for many years without changes or updates. I worked for one organisation that updated policies yearly and "required" all employees to read and agree to the updates. As they found no way to enforce this, senior staff members could ignore the updates and never respond without consequence. The rest of the staff could therefore do the same.

Policies should include detailed explanations of the consequences for those who break the rules. The penalties must be enforced.

> "We need to move from a mentality of producing evidence-based policy to one of creating policy-based evidence" (John List[72])

Different policies are probably necessary and should combine to explain the required attitudes and ethics.

Policies do not explain how things are done in detail but define expectations as diverse as dress code, data protection, recycling, respect of standards, and more.

---

[72] "The Voltage Effect" ISBN 9780241556849

Policies should only change rarely. They do not depend on people, projects, tools, technology, processes or fashions but guide them. A policy explicitly refers to the need to respect it and the penalties related to violations.

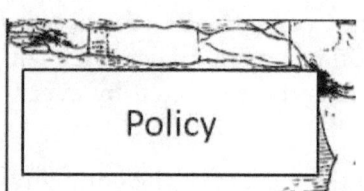

The VQ illustration represents the policy on one of the hands. This position highlights the idea that the policy is management's right hand, a practical foundation of the organisation. Its role is to complete the vision and mission statements by defining *why* something needs to be done.

16.2.3 Strategy

On the other side of the VQ man, we find the strategy. While the mission and vision statements establish the

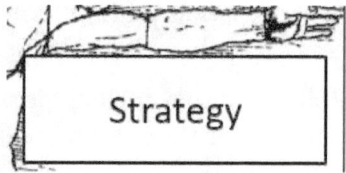

long-term objectives of the organisation and the policy defines why something needs to be done, the strategy starts the practical aspect of the organisation of tasks.

The strategy supports the mission and vision statements; it links them to quantifiable goals and milestones when the effects and results should be seen and felt by the customers and staff members.

While the mission and vision statements define overall concepts, the strategy clarifies the steps leading to their implementation.

The strategy may include timelines but should not become a plan with milestones. Its focus should be more on dependencies and priorities than timeframes and calendars. It is a general plan to achieve the organisation's long-term goals, and it must take into account the uncertainties of the future. Your strategy should not fail because you missed a deadline.

16.2.4 Training

"What if I train them and they leave?" asks the director. "What if you don't train them and they stay?" replies the instructor.

Training is in the centre of your business as it is in the centre of the VQ image. It is the centre of gravity of your business, and everything depends on it working correctly.

Training is needed throughout everyone's career; you need it to remain fresh, learn new techniques, and understand new possibilities. Without training, you may be applying techniques and solutions that are outdated and inefficient and lose out to your competitors as they remain at the cutting edge of technology.

Training need not have to be expensive or intrusive. Internal training, cross-fertilisation and mentoring are practical, valuable and useful. I have met, in my career, at least two organisations that ran into serious difficulty by not focusing sufficiently on internal training. In both cases, one employee had critically important knowledge that was not shared; the employee decided to leave and create an independent company based on that knowledge. Customers were left with little doubt about whom to follow if they wanted answers to their problems.

The vision gave us goals and told us what to achieve.

The policies established the non-negotiable aspects and explained why things had to be done.

The strategy laid out the organisation and dependencies and outlined when to do things.

Training tells us how to do it. Its purpose is to instruct people on how to use technology, apply procedures or use tools efficiently. It involves showing the usage and the results so they can rapidly become standard working practices.

16.2.5 Process

The process defines *what* needs to be done.

Processes complete the picture. Each policy probably has several related processes supporting it.

I frequently find confusion between "process" and "procedure" concepts. The process should establish what needs to be done, but not how or who is supposed to do it. A process will state that something needs to be "communicated" but should not tell you to use the phone, email or documentation. If several processes support each policy, likewise, several procedures will support each process.

The processes establish clear objectives, outcomes and products; it illustrates high-level dataflows. A process may typically cover the need to review all documents before publication but will not explain how or by whom – the details are in the corresponding procedures.

A process should include several characteristics to establish its perennity. These include:

- The consumables: what is needed and in what state before the work can begin;
- The products: what will be the outcome of the process, and how it is validated as finalised;

- Sequential activities that are needed to transform the data, product and service from start to end;
- Identification of key stakeholders, particularly the "customer" (the person who depends on this being completed) and the "supplier" (the person on whom the team depends to start);
- Major controls to be used to manage the process while it is being run: measurements, verification and validation activities or tools, templates, standards and others.

A process should not change too frequently. It is defined so that changes in staffing, organisation, tools, technology, training or procedures should not impact it significantly.

Procedures will fill in the details of each process, defining *how* things are done. These may frequently change whenever there is a variation in the context.

Processes need to remain unchanged but have flexibility built into them. They must allow the organisation to progress while remaining structured in its offering. Like the knees, they combine these varied functions, supporting the work while offering stability and flexibility.

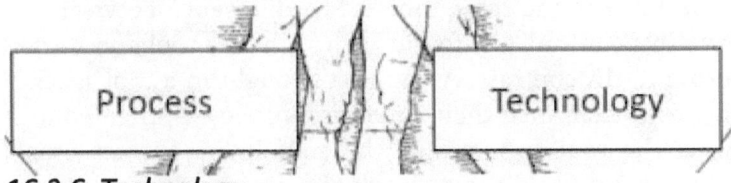

16.2.6 Technology

Like processes, technologies need to support the work, remain flexible and offer stability and continuity.

The word "technology" is frequently only considered as relating to electronics, software and hardware. The term should be considered in a broader sense to include tools of various sorts, such as templates and standards, tools and equipment. Technology is vital in most activities (or should I say all activities?)

The objective of technology is to facilitate the work being done. Good technology should make it easier and faster to produce good quality, it eases the tasks for the individuals and makes their life better.

Every technology, like every process, will create additional tasks. These need to be understood and justified. Training is provided to help individuals involved know that the extra activities are not bureaucracies but serve an essential purpose over the life of the product or activities. If I need to spend an additional hour documenting what I have done, I need to be reassured that this is saving more than one hour's effort somewhere down the line.

Many organisations and team members quickly complain about technology and blame it for any shortcomings. One of my former customers compared results between two sites and determined that a tool used at site A was obviously better than the one at site B. As the team from site B went over to investigate what they had implemented, they found it was the same tool. The difference between the two installations was found. B bought the tool and started using it. In contrast, A had first brought in a tool specialist, who examined their needs and processes, then configured the tool and trained the staff in its correct usage. Many good tools and technologies are poorly implemented, leading to frustration and additional work. Having already invested in the purchase, management does not see the value in spending more money on a consultant.

The technology, if correctly applied, should facilitate and speed up the implementation of the required procedures and activities.

Technologies should not be purchased or implemented without a good understanding of how they fit into the organisation and the role they are supposed to fulfil. Most frequently, professional assistance to set them up in the most effective manner is of great value.

16.2.7 Continuous Improvement

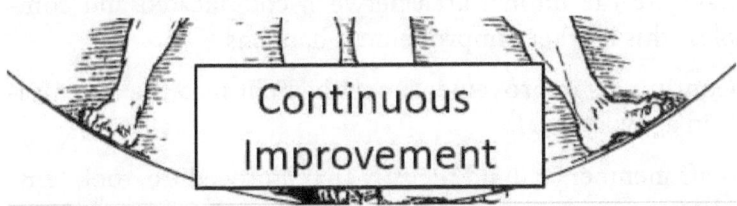

There is a discussion to be had here, and I have long hesitated on the right word to use:

- Continuous means that this goes on without interruption, like the flow of the tides;
- Continual means that this happens on an ongoing basis, regularly, in phases.

You might therefore prefer continual improvement to what I have put here. You would appreciate regular releases of new practices, software and products that allow improvement. But you would baulk at continuous improvement, implying that tasks are being improved while you perform them.

I remain with "continuous improvement" because my focus is the organisation, not your local activity or task.

Continuous improvement forms the feet of the VQ schema because they are the most critical aspect of supporting you as you move forward.

When you walk, you first need to lean forward and get out

of balance; you then move a foot forward to catch yourself and avoid falling on your face.

The same principle applies to continuous improvement, in which you stretch the organisation to be slightly out of balance and implement the improvement. Referring back to the Cynefin framework[73], you want to avoid remaining in the "obvious[74]" quadrant. Instead, you should try to navigate the liminal area between complicated and complex: this is where improvement happens.

Continuous improvement must be built into the organisation at every level.

Staff members should identify that a procedure, tool, template, or way of working does not meet expectations or could be refined and improved. You will always find waste and redundancy if you look; the idea here is that the people best placed to identify these can do it. Rather than obliging them to follow step-by-step procedures, they need to have a detailed understanding of what is essential: the mission and vision statements, the desired results of a process, the dependencies outlined in the strategy, and the training to understand the values and costs.

Continuous improvement and education[75] are closely related.

Team members should remain focused on the goal of their process rather than on the task they are performing. They must be encouraged to identify missing steps or data or

---

[73] See page 75.
[74] Someone once said that the Obvious quadrant was where cash-cows go to die.
[75] See paragraph 16.3.2 on Feedback, page 9.

recommend shortcuts that do not result in a loss of value.

The continuous improvement concept is implemented at several levels:

- A formal performance improvement team has the responsibility and authority for collecting, structuring, testing and deploying proposed improvements and changes;
- "Lessons learnt"[76] are conducted regularly with the team members, allowing them to identify any aspect that has gone wrong and the causes of any particular success;
- Progress review and team meetings capture impediments, risks and issues systematically and in a standardised format; team leaders must communicate these and their resolutions when appropriate.

Of course, a continuous improvement programme cannot be truly effective if you don't have the environmental support necessary to allow participants to express themselves and act appropriately.

---

[76] These sessions aim at learning lessons and identifying improvements for both the team and the whole organisation. Too frequently teams conduct some sort of session during which they complain about everything that went wrong, but don't learn any lessons. Sessions should also include lessons on what went well and how this can be reproduced.

16.3   The Circle

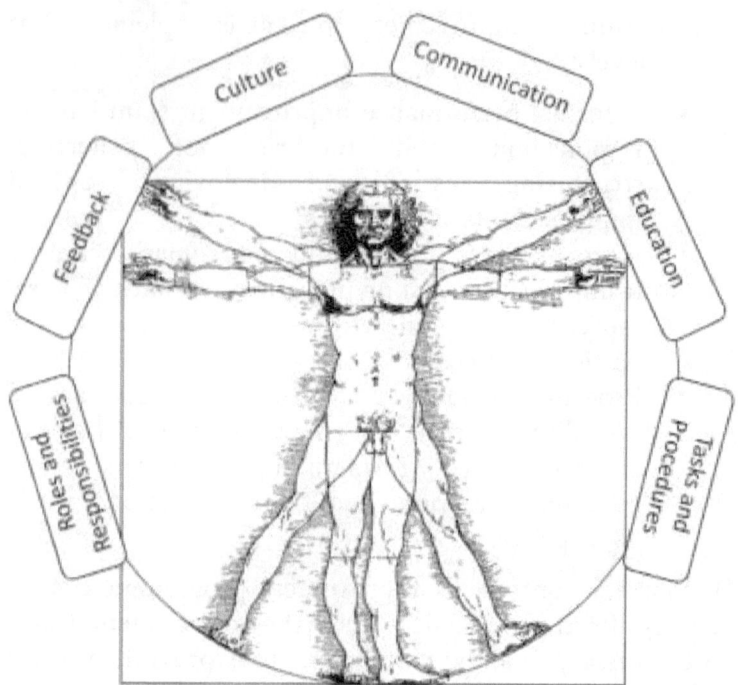

The circle seeks to cover the "soft skills" necessary for team members to work correctly. These areas are too frequently forgotten by management in their efforts to manage.

While the "square" activities are critical to the good conduct of operations and the primary role of management, the following are frequently forgotten as they are too obvious and taken for granted.

16.3.1 Roles and Responsibilities

Starting at the bottom left of the circle, we have the idea that people need to be given roles and responsibilities in the organisation. Bizarrely, many organisations appear to forget how important this is and just hire people who may have some technical knowledge to fill the role.

This activity has two steps: defining the role and assigning it to the right individual.

16.3.1.1 Defining the Roles
Many organisations continue to believe that they need to establish a hierarchical organisation that matches those of traditional business structures.

I recommend considering that perhaps your organisation could be different. Let's first define the needs of the organisation and what are the roles and structures needed. The organisation's purpose is to build a product or deliver a service; many things need to be in place to achieve the desired results. Traditionally, departments are rapidly created for many of these when they could be done better by the team members directly. Consider the traditional responsibilities of the human resources (HR) department:

- Recruitment of Candidates
- Payroll Processing
- Policies of the Workplace
- Training and Development
- Performance Reviews and Promotion of the Employees

You probably need someone who understands and can process payrolls, including the necessary taxes and reports. However, (in my opinion) that is essentially an accounting activity, no more or less complicated

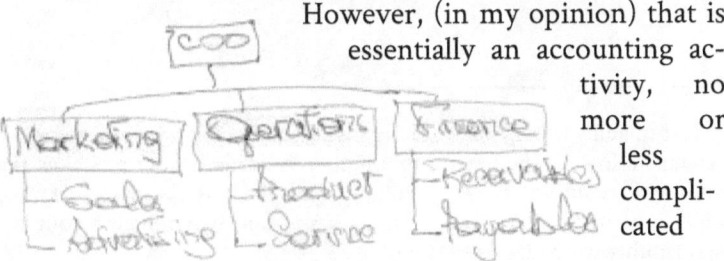

than invoicing and paying debts. The teams should manage recruiting, training, and performance reviews directly. When recruiting, finding an individual who can work with the team and perform the required activities is essential. You do not expect an HR specialist to understand your team's technical needs or judge suitability from a cultural point of view. The team itself should be able to identify what training is required and who could use it best.

Once the roles have been identified, the corresponding responsibilities (and authority) should be laid out in the same organisational chart. Your responsibilities, authority[77], and accountability should be obvious when you fill a position.

Consider the smallest number of roles without which the business cannot survive and define those. Then identify which of these roles will require assistance, either specialist knowledge or practical implementation and work on those. If you are the CEO, GM, or Director of a business with more than twenty employees (or the leader of an equally large team), you should acknowledge that your focus is to work *on* the business and not *in* the business. This new focus is a significant hurdle for many entrepreneurs as they understand that they must choose. You either run the company or work on the tasks you enjoyed and made your first success.

---

[77] Just to add a note: you can delegate authority; you never delegate the responsibility. If the person to whom you delegate does not have the authority required, they cannot perform what is required. If they don't have the skills or competencies and fail, that remains your responsibility for badly delegating.

16.3.1.2 Assigning a Role

Finding the right person to fill a role demands some work. You need to identify the skills and knowledge necessary, of course. However, it is more important to determine which are required from the start and which can be acquired by the person concerned.

A mistake that many people make is to work on hiring people who "will fit in with the team". They form teams of people with similar backgrounds, education, and interests, assuming that creating a cohesive team will lead to success.

No matter how skilled you are, you only know a small portion of everything there is to know on any given topic. By forming a "cohesive" team of clones, you are only creating a significant amount of redundant knowledge and experience. This team continues only to know the same small portion. You want to include people of different backgrounds[78] who will bring another form of knowledge or experience. Maybe they don't know as much as you learned from your doctorate, but they might have real-

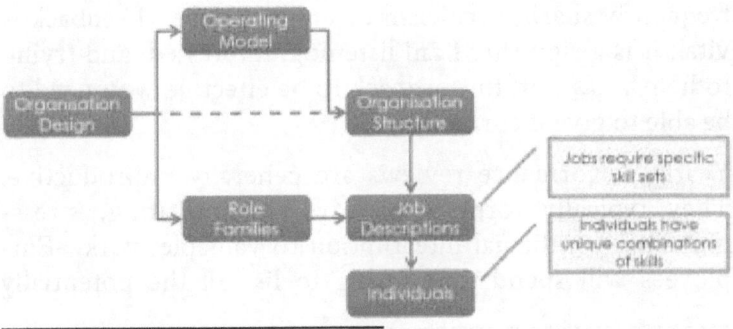

---

[78] In "backgrounds", I am including race, age, economic, social, sexual and gender, physical abilities and more.

world experience that complements it.

Within the knowledge-based industries, I like SFIA[79]. This framework lists over one hundred skills habitual in modern businesses. Each skill is then given up to seven, based on abilities, experience, competencies, and education. This construct allows you to identify all the necessary or recommended skills for a given role and who has experience, knowledge, or potential.

Once a role has been defined, with responsibility and authority defined, it is important to respect what was agreed. Even as CEO, you should not publicly overrule your managers, you do not bypass them to communicate with their team, and you do not make decisions that are part of their remit (more about this in section 16.3.4, page 141).

Respect the authority and responsibilities, but do not hesitate to give alternate ideas and corrections.

16.3.2 Feedback
Employees are frequently told when they make a mistake, rarely when they have done something well.

Some people are afraid of giving feedback; others are too frequently sharing criticism or empty praise. Feedback is vital: it is a sign that I am listening, interested, and trying to help you. But, for feedback to be effective, you need to be able to give it correctly.

Yearly performance reviews are generally unproductive. They typically form a negative, demotivating, stress-inducing, conflictual interruption to valuable work. Employees will spend time trying to list all the potentially

---

[79] The "Skills Framework for the Information Age", more from https://www.sfia-online.org.

good things they have done over the past year. This activity is seen as necessary to demonstrate why they should get a promotion or a raise. Because the employees are overly optimistic, managers are required to shoot down their egos, point out all the mistakes made, and tell them why they cannot have more money or a promotion –they are even lucky to continue being employed. After some routine discussion back and forth, they agree on what was already decided in an earlier budget meeting.

Due to its yearly occurrence, most things that should be included are forgotten, and activities of the past couple of months take on unwarranted importance.

Good feedback is essential. It allows mistakes to be corrected rapidly and progress to be made. There are broadly two types of feedback.

- Positive: congratulate someone on a job well done. If delivered correctly[80], this gives a nice warm feeling for a few minutes; otherwise, it has no value.
- Constructive: help identify areas of failure or insufficiency and recommend actionable improvement. If you are only criticising, this is demoralising. However, if you turn it into something actionable, it is beneficial.

Feedback is essential, both positive and negative, as rapidly as possible to ensure that lessons are learnt and corrections are implemented in real-time.

---

[80] I worked for a former air force man, who believed that coming out of his office on a regular basis and saying "good job, chaps, keep it up" would be sufficient.

For feedback to be truly effective, it needs:

- To be given in a spirit of trying to improve or reinforce an attitude or capability, and
- Received gratefully, recognising that the person providing feedback is trying to help, not abuse or humiliate.

In this context, any feedback should be welcome. It would be best if you learned to welcome input from all concerned: manager, colleague, or employee. As CEO, you should listen, acknowledge, and accept the feedback given to you by someone with no authority in the organisation. As a team member, you should actively request feedback from your colleagues.

This level of comment and input need not be formalised but must be accepted. Until you are confident that you have established complete trust, you may want to implement a process for anonymous comments.

16.3.3 Culture

As mentioned elsewhere, an organisation's culture is people's attitude when no one is watching.

It covers the things that team members consider "natural", "normal", or "obvious". Culture is frequently the result of many factors that are no longer noticeable but taken for granted.

Understanding the culture requires an external point of view to establish the reality that no one notices. Just as the fish does not know about water, the people in the organisation frequently do not understand the fundamental attitude problems impacting their effectiveness.

Two approaches are recommended to understand the culture and its weaknesses:

- Interviews by an external consultant[81] able to identify through experience things that may be less normal than believed – this approach is helpful to get things started but is not recommended as an ongoing practice;
- Requiring new starters to make a free-format public presentation about what surprised them in the organisation. Doing this after four to six months highlights aspects you no longer notice but are not considered habitual to outsiders.

The cultural aspects should stress the organisation's values: do the team members have the same understanding as the executive? They should also highlight the trust required between the individuals concerned.

The best indicator of the culture is found in informal communication.

16.3.4 Communication

> *If no one is listening, you are not communicating.*

Somewhere in the world, there may be an organisation where employees are not complaining about communication. Still, if it exists, it is probably unique.

Communication must be organised formally and encouraged informally. It needs to combine active and passive attributes.

---

[81] One of the main advantages of external consultants is that they are usually allowed to say things to management that would not be tolerated from employees.

I have frequently encountered the same negative attitude to communication.

- I am a good communicator. If you need something and come ask me, I will be happy to share it with you;
- You are a poor communicator. If I need something, you don't share unless I specifically come to ask you about it.

Many appear to believe this without seeing the inherent contradictions due to the emphasis always placed on the other person.

16.3.4.1 Formal Communication

The active part of communication is the more challenging: you need to communicate to everyone the information they need without overloading them. The best form of communication is probably still face-to-face. This means going to people to talk to them without hiding behind electronic applications.

The passive side involves setting up a process, system or methodology that allows people to find the information rapidly and easily they need when they need it. Many applications[82] support this. As with so many others, parametrisation and set-up are the main issues with these applications. They seek to answer so many needs that they can rapidly get overly complex. Setting them up and enforcing the rules is a critical step before trying to use them.

16.3.4.2 Informal Communication

One of the significant failures of the age of electronic

---

[82] Microsoft's SharePoint, Meta's Workplace, Atlassian's Confluence to name three.

meetings is the absence of serendipity. When as an average employee, you went to the coffee machine (or water cooler) and happened to meet someone with whom you have no official exchanges. You start chatting with the CEO, with the IT guy, with the cleaner. These random meetings are impossible on Zoom, Teams, WebEx or GoToMeeting, for which appointments must be scheduled.

Previously, we had a different problem. Most organisations remained convinced that they should have open-plan offices, even though no one has managed to prove any value[83]. Because of the ambient noise in an open-plan office, many team members isolate themselves with earphones; others are continuously distracted and interrupted by the noise and conversations of their colleagues. Getting the balance right is an art in itself.

Roles and responsibilities have been defined, and now they must be respected. While it is good to encourage informal conversations between all levels and teams within the organisation, you may never bypass the "chain of command".

If you are the director, you do not give instructions to team members without their manager being aware and agreeing. You should never openly contradict a department head or team leader in front of their reports. Suppose employees bypass the chain of command and go to a senior executive with something rather than their direct manager. In that case, the executive needs to bring the manager into the conversation.

---

[83] The only real value is for the people who need to reorganise the office space on a regular basis.

16.3.5 Education

While training is (sometimes) included in organisations' offerings, education is frequently ignored.

Training teaches people *how* to do things (how to use a tool, how to follow a process), and education teaches people *why*. Education prepares you to think for yourself by understanding and focusing on the purpose and the end goals instead of only the sequence of tasks.

Through an effort in education, team members and managers can spend more time doing what matters to the business and the customers. They can identify the weaknesses in the system and recommend valuable improvements.

One robust approach to education is found in coaching. Coaching is not improvised; it is not just showing people how to follow the guidelines. It is trying to get them to understand the reasons behind decisions and how to collect the data required to make a good decision. My preferred approach is Toyota's A3 methodology, in which a manager encourages and challenges a team member to go back and ask better questions[84].

The basic concept of an A3 approach is to get someone to bring everything down to the fundamental principles succinctly enough to fit on a single sheet of paper (A3 or double the standard printer paper size). The information on this sheet includes the problem statement, root causes, consequences, proposed corrective actions, subsequent

---

[84] John Shook explains and demonstrates this method very well in his book "Managing to Learn", in which he focuses on the manager's responsibility to encourage learning in team members. See page 144 for an A3 template.

follow-up and controls.

A different aspect of education is ensuring that every team member understands what you have done to cover all the preceding points in this chapter. Your team members need to understand the organisational mission and vision statements, the policies and strategy, their responsibility for continuous improvement, how to give feedback, and the rest.

> *Give them the power to be empowered.*

16.3.6 Tasks and Procedures

Once the structure is in place, the people on the front line, the factory floor, need to understand how their daily activities, tasks and procedures fit into the big picture.

Too frequently, a patriarchal tendency encourages functional stupidity, forcing team members to do as they are told "because I say so".

In an intelligence-based industry[85], with a team of people hired because they are intelligent and can think for themselves, you should not force them into mindless obedience. They must understand how their little corner of the corporate puzzle completes the picture and believe they are making a difference.

They need to know your company's mission statement and believe in it. They need to trust that their activities are actively helping achieve that mission. They need to understand how all the different pieces fit together and trust

---

[85] Most industries should now be intelligence based, only a few sweat-shops can still rely on brain-dead interchangeable workers repeating gestures endlessly.

that their contribution, whether in their daily routine or recommendations for continual improvement, is appreciated.

Tasks and procedures are essential in every industry; they are most effective when the people involved in performing the activities are directly implicated in defining them.

You want to go beyond management: you want to be a leader. You want to be someone who is respected, listened to, and whom people want to follow and emulate.

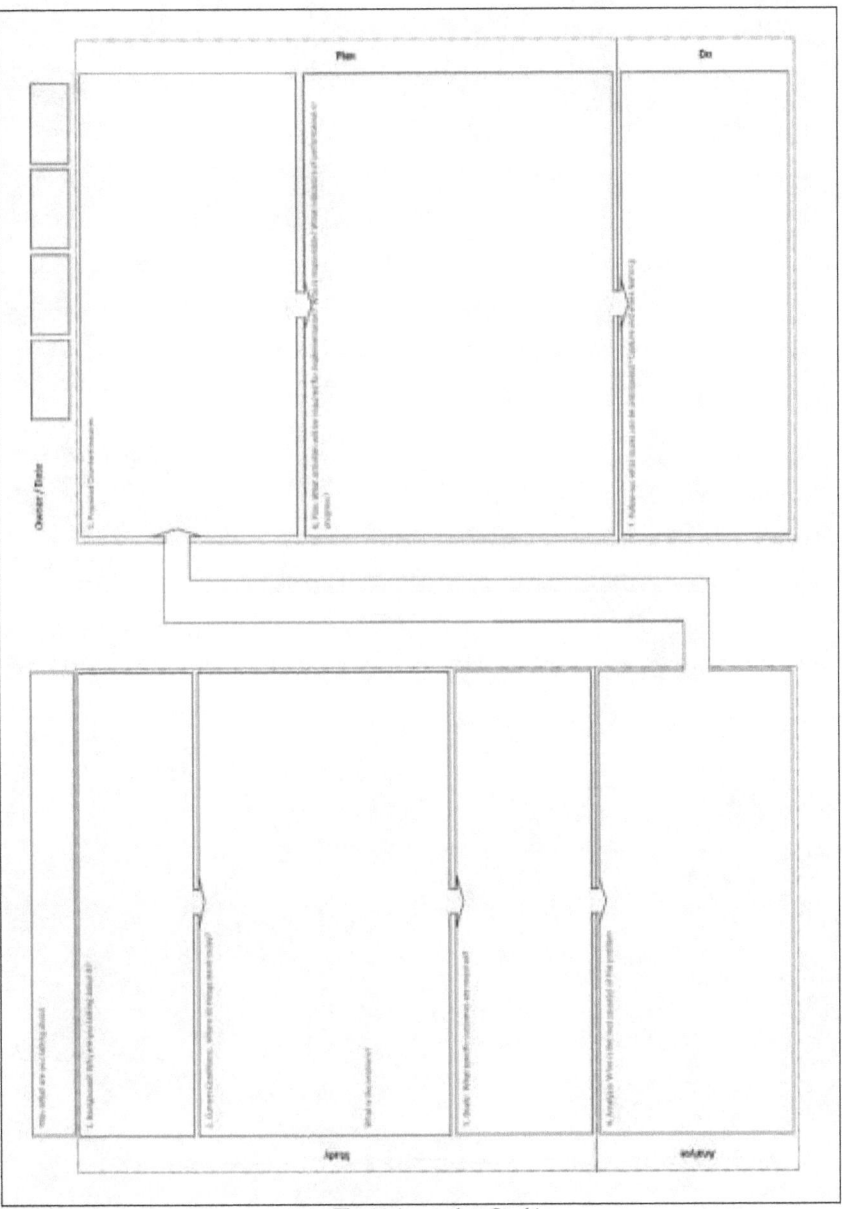

16-2 - The A3 Approach to Coaching

17 Management and Leadership

Over the past few years, the need for management has changed quite a lot. This change has been primarily due to the lockdowns that started in 2020, following the outbreak of Covid-19. The lockdowns allowed a better understanding of who could work remotely and who remains a critical front-line worker.

17.1 Manager or Leader?

17.1.1 Cautionary Tale

In June 1910, two men led their crews to the South Pole, hoping to be the first to arrive. Captain Robert Scott set out from England, Roald Amundsen from Norway.

Scott was well equipped, well-financed and had the backing of the British Navy. He carried some of the best modern technology available and a large crew. His backers had given him instructions on how to behave in proper English heroic fashion and what they wanted to get out of the expedition to the last unchartered area of the world.

Amundsen set out from the newly independent Norway in the middle of the night. He told his backers and crew they were going to the Arctic and only changed the instructions to go South once he was at sea.

The stories of both crews are well documented and known. When Scott arrived at the South Pole, he found the Norwegian flag already in position.

Should you want more details on what happened and why it all happened this way, I can heartily recommend listening to the retelling of their stories by Tim Harford in his podcast "Cautionary Tales."[86]

As I listened to the story of the two men, I concluded that Scott was a good manager while Amundsen was a good leader. They were very different men, with very different objectives and methods. They both achieved remarkable successes, but only a leader could be the first to reach the South Pole.

The terms are frequently confused when talking about management but also by managers who believe themselves to be leaders.

> *You must obey a manager;*
> *you want to follow a leader.*

17.1.2 The Manager

The manager is someone who understands the current situation. The manager is aware of the budget, progress, policies, levels of absenteeism, and a lot more. A manager seeks to move the team forward without creating trouble or rocking the boat.

Critical roles for a manager include:

- Maintaining an objective perspective from behind the troops,

---

[86] Cautionary Tales, season 3, episodes dated July 15 (David and Goliath on Ice), July 29 ("Mummy is Amundsen a Good Man") and August 12, 2022 (When the Limeys Get Scurvy).

- Establishing the environment and the infrastructure that allows team members to do their best,
- Creating an atmosphere that facilitates collaboration and reflects executive objectives,
- Enabling productivity and performance enhancement through tools and processes,
- Establishing priorities for team members as well as for the entire team,
- Encouraging and promoting stability,
- Communicating and defending the business interests of the organisations,
- Getting things done and ensuring progress,
- Controlling the team and ensuring that everyone is doing their job,
- Sharing information about the team to the hierarchy and from the executive to the team,
- Keeping documentation up to date.

17.1.3 The Leader
Leaders are people with a vision. They are determined to reach their goal and will overturn tables and crash through walls to achieve their dream. Many great businesspeople were leaders who wanted to achieve something and overcame all obstacles to get to their goal. The single-minded ruthlessness of the approach may lead you to believe that they were unkind and uncaring and stepped on many people on their way[87] to the top.

A good leader's roles include:

- Charging in front of the troops, good leaders would not force anyone to go anywhere ahead of

---

[87] And indubitably so of them are.

them or send them somewhere they are not ready to go themselves,

- Communicating a vision in terms that inspire,

- Motivating team members to buy into the dream, the vision,

- Encouraging people,

- Building enthusiasm for the future,

- Encouraging and liking movement – anything is better than the status quo,

- Sharing and being interested in personal interests,

- Doing things, practical, tangible things,

- Leading so that others follow,

- Sharing knowledge with and from others.

17.1.4 Confusing

In the coming section, I am going to contradict myself somewhat and conflate management and leadership. I will use the term "manager" to refer to the person in charge of getting the best out of a group of people. In general, I believe that managers and leaders are very different people and have very different roles and objectives. Unfortunately, the text rapidly becomes confusing and unreadable if I need to be precise at every reference.

By fusing these two roles in the next section, I am talking about someone who has combined the motivation for future expansion with stabilising the budget. Imagine a politician who delivers on their electoral promises and succeeds in reducing taxes while increasing social benefits – an unlikely combination which, somehow, we have come to expect.

Management must evolve with the team to guide them and encourage continuous growth.

17.2   Four Types of Management

Team management and team leadership are frequently needed at different levels. Teams, when they come together, typically go through varying levels of collaboration, often referred to as:

- **Form**: the group is created, and members are wondering why they are there and what is the objective of this new collaboration;
- **Storm**: team members start measuring each other up and are still in a self-defence mode, questioning why decisions are made by another team member and demanding that their personal skills be better recognised and respected – often trusting their own skills to be greater than they are;
- **Norm**: the members have understood their role and are doing their job; they accept tasks and produce results as expected;
- **Perform**: team members recognise and defer to the skills of their colleagues; they surrender tasks to others who can perform them better or faster, accepting that some jobs are assigned to them without warning.

As the team progresses, performance increases in parallel with recognising the team's value and respect for others.

As the team progresses through these different levels, management must evolve in their attitude.

17.2.1 Directing the Formed Team
A newly formed team needs direction.

Management needs to define outcomes, plan activities, and assign individual tasks.

At this point, team members are trying to identify what they are supposed to do and need the encouragement of solid management to give them clear instructions and expectations.

Management needs to combine their planning activities with an effort to teach team members. They must show them what needs to be done and how to do it efficiently. They must assign tasks and continually verify, check, control, and validate the results.

The team has to define itself; team members must understand what is expected of them. The manager needs to expect failure and short-comings, and encourage team members, show them how to resolve the issues as and when they occur

17.2.2 Coaching the Storming Team
Team members will try to impose themselves, demonstrate their value and challenge their colleagues. In school and the workplace, there is pressure to compete. The individuals are pressured to show themselves as better, faster, and smarter than others. Only the best arrives first. When placed in a team, the competitive attitude is dominant. Team members must be coached into accepting the team as the better option.

They have been to the best schools; they have experience and knowledge. Why should they submit themselves to the judgement or authority of a colleague?

The storming phase of a team is one of the more difficult phases of management. Traditional planning and monitoring techniques are not enough, and you need to focus on social, soft skills, and the ability to negotiate.

Things heat up, individuals get into arguments, and managers wonder why they were ever considered to be on this team. However, they must demonstrate patience and empathy, exploring and seeking out real issues that provoke outbursts. They need to learn to listen, understand, and act accordingly to bring peace and enthusiasm to the team.

Now is when the skills of Conflict Transformation[88] come into play to transform the energy of a conflict into a powerful motor of continual improvement. Team members must be praised and encouraged at this time to continue to believe in the team.

Coaching, handholding, and understanding are the keywords in this phase of team management.

17.2.3 Supporting the Normal Team
The team has found its cruising speed. It is now producing results, team members understand their role and the value of (some) colleagues, and they are progressing at a steady pace.

Possibly the easiest time for management who can relax their vigilance slightly and focus more on supporting the team members' capability to solve their own issues. Mistakes will be made, and encouragement and support are needed. The manager now needs to be able to deliver and receive feedback[89].

The purpose of feedback is to assist; it is not to blame or destroy. Feedback should be aimed at helping the managers support their team members' efforts and guide them in

---

[88] See section 6.3 on Conflict Transformation, page 38.
[89] See section 16.3.2 on Feedback, page 136.

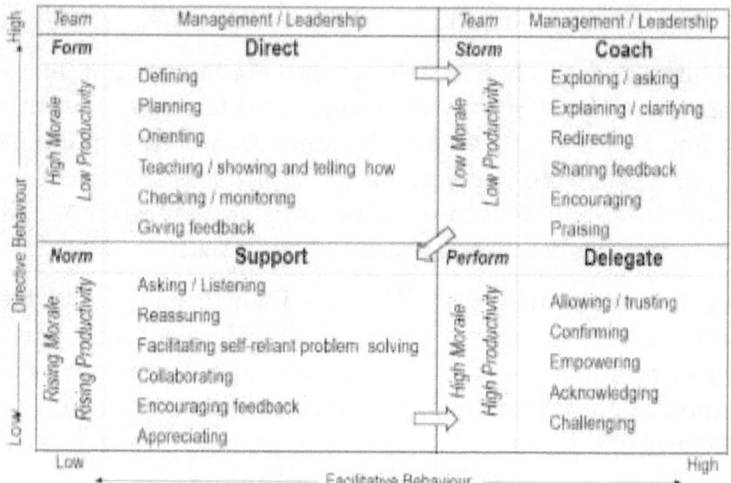

the prioritisation of tasks.

17.2.4 Delegating to the Performing Team

The team has now reached the point of mutual trust and knowledge. Members know who is best at various tasks and can determine the best approach to solving issues. Collaboration allows them to automatically assign tasks, questions, and decisions to the most appropriate person from the team's point of view.

Leadership is now at its most demanding: there is no more a need for management to tell individuals and teams what to do, how to do it or when. Measurement, supervision, and controls are reduced to a strict minimum. What is needed is delegation, mutual trust, confirming and affirming.

At this point, the most challenging aspect of leadership is the team members' continuous need for individual challenges.

It may be surprising that people need a reasonable amount

of stress to be efficient.

Suppose you join a tennis club, and you are, by far, the worst player in the club. No matter whom you are playing, you lose hopelessly. Before long, you will give up on tennis as you are no good at it. Now, suppose you are the very best player in the club and trounce all the others every time. Before long, you will lose interest and realise you cannot progress any further.

As a leader of a performing team, your focus must be on continually stretching your team members sufficiently to allow them to grow, but not to breaking point.

17.3 Hybrid Management

Since 2020, the notion of hybrid teams has taken a big step forward. In such a team, one needs to be aware of the needs and advantages of having team members working in the office and others working from home. In such an environment, the manager/leader faces a new, or increased, series of demands and expectations.

Traditional skills that a good manager is expected to demonstrate include:

- Communicate
  o With the team
  o With each team member
  o With other stakeholders (management, customers, suppliers, other project managers)
- Leadership by example
- Inspire and Motivate
- Conflict transformation
- Team development

- Mentoring
- Negotiation
- Troubleshooting
- Estimating, planning and bidding
- Matching external competitive drivers and internal capabilities
- Monitoring and Tracking

In addition to these, hybrid management needs to develop the following skills:

- Adjustment to change
- Ambiguity Management
- Change Management
- Conflict transformation
- Collaboration
- Compassion
- Curiosity
- Motivating people
- Different forms of intelligence
- Knowledge management
- Psychology and Sociology

Let me go through some details.

17.3.1 Adjustment
Within a hybrid context, the manager needs, more than ever, to remain calm under pressure and control their own stress levels and those of their team.

To achieve this, I remember that:

> *"Peace of mind isn't at all superficial,*
> *really. It's the whole thing."*[90]

Without peace of mind, you cannot perform effectively. Achieving peace of mind requires some adaptations to the way you act:

- Don't worry; think instead
- When everything falls apart or changes
  - o Take a deep breath
  - o Examine the causes and consequences
  - o Decide how to proceed
- It's not a problem; it's a challenge.

17.3.2 Ambiguity Management

Managers need, more than ever, to learn how to deal with complex and contradictory information to achieve the best result.

Over the past few years, the world has appeared to move more towards extremes. Through the power of social media, extremists of all kinds express their opinions loudly and repeatedly. This extremism is true in politics more than before, but it is also in many other areas. Online arguments between the defenders and opponents of vaccination, abortion, border control and others are raging. Meanwhile, most moderates do not see their opinions expressed publicly and feel isolated, even if they form

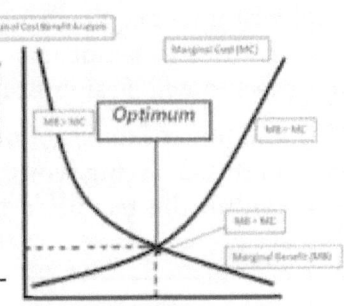

---

[90] From "Zen and the Art of Motorcycle Maintenance" ©1974 Robert Pirsig.

the majority.

In organisations, a vigorous discussion exists about the relative productivity of working from home or in the office. The truth lies, as always, somewhere in the middle and is mainly dependent on the context and the individual.

In your team, you will probably have introverts and extroverts, the ones who need social interaction and those who need solitude to "recharge". Deciding whether the team should come together needs to consider both groups.

This dilemma can be compared to the traditional manager's role as an arbitrator between the customer. the executive, and the team members[91].

17.3.3 Change Management

Disruption is the new constant. Changes in the environment, legislation, international trade, customer opinions, competition, and team membership work together to make the manager's job more difficult.

It is the manager's job to remain aware of potential changes in context so they can attempt to smooth transitions continuously.

Remember that every change, whether in team membership, customer requirements or international politics, is a risk. If the risk is not managed appropriately, it becomes an issue and will be significantly more challenging.

17.3.4 Conflict Transformation

Within this changing world, we will encounter many conflicts within the team and between the team and outside

---

[91] You need more time, but you want it faster; you need more investment, but you want it cheaper.

influences. Most frequently, these conflicts are slow-growing antipathies that originate in a difference that may appear trivial: a difference in communication styles, learning capabilities, or political opinions. These form the most significant risks in any team and typically only get taken seriously when something breaks.

When conflict occurs, it is the manager's role to identify the actual cause. The manager should not just react to the event but find out what happened over time and why it snapped at this point.

Conflict management and conflict resolution frequently involve either ignoring the cause of the conflict or imposing a solution that pleases no one. Conflict transformation is working with the conflictual situation to determine how to transform this energy into something that serves the team. For more on this topic, see section 6.3, page 39.

We are quick to judge and jump to conclusions. As a manager, your first step in a conflict must be to examine your own thinking.

17.3.5 Collaboration
Beyond all the techniques and principles, managing a team is mostly an exercise in communication. A rapid analysis of the communication channels quickly shows the issue.

While only two flows of communication can go wrong between two people (me to you and you to me), that number snowballs, giving us six flows for three people and twelve for just four people.

  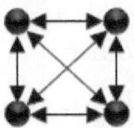

A relatively small team of eight has 56 different communication flows between team members! If one of these fails, if one team member does not listen or share information appropriately with one other, the whole team can collapse and fail in its mission.

When considering the changing number of team members working alone or remotely, even with all the possibilities of electronic communications, this problem gets magnified.

17.3.6 Compassion

Because of this new environment, the need for compassion is felt more accurately.

In the past, requiring people to be at their workstations for a set number of hours daily was easy. They were expected to show up and be at work, notwithstanding issues in commuting or family circumstances. Remote work highlights new problems: a family crisis, a sick child, or a local power failure can disrupt the work unexpectedly. I can take a break to do some shopping or gardening – should I be penalised for this? People working from home may start work at 6:00 in the morning by checking their emails before breakfast. They might only finish after 22:00. The workday is redefined when your home becomes your office – it can sometimes be challenging to determine whether you are working from home or sleeping at the office.

If you require team members to be available and at work

during traditional work hours, you must ensure they are taking time off outside those hours. Working ten hours a day or seven days a week is a significant cause of physical and mental health problems.

Working long hours increases the number of errors made.

Managers need to keep an eye on the mental health of their team. When working in an office, you can see someone is depressed and not participating. However, when you only see them in scheduled, online team meetings, it becomes more challenging to identify the person who is not participating.

17.3.7 Curiosity

Many of these issues can be solved by encouraging managers to be curious. Please find out about your team members' families, ask about their relationships, and keep notes. Ask them about their work environment when working from home: do they have access to a proper desk with reasonable ergonomic standards? Are they working in a quiet environment? Do they have appropriate heating and cooling systems to maintain acceptable comfort levels while working from home? Do they need assistance in setting up a home office?

You cannot expect team members to produce acceptable levels of quality work while sitting on a couch with a laptop. They cannot concentrate at a kitchen table when they have to move everything away three times a day.

One of the basic principles of agnotology[92] is encouraging

---

[92] The study of deliberate or culturally induced ignorance. The book "Agnotology" by Robert Proctor and Londa Schiebinger (2008) covers this in detail.

you to find out what you don't know and *why* you don't know. What are people deliberately trying to hide from you?

A classic example of this can be found in most organisations' HR departments:

- Did you conduct an exit review when X left?
- Yes, we always interview them before they leave.
- What was the main reason for X leaving the company?
- She was offered more money somewhere else.

Maybe X was a world-renowned specialist who got headhunted. In most cases, if someone is offered more money (or more responsibility, or better working hours, or whatever), they are actively looking for another job and applying for interviews. Why is HR not interested or courageous enough to discover and communicate the reason for the person's disaffection?

17.3.8 Motivation
Your first responsibility is to ensure your team members want to complete and deliver their work according to established constraints (quality, schedule, budget).

People want to take pride in their work. As a manager, you should be focused on removing any and all obstacles to their natural desire to be proud of their work.

In the past, too many managers have focused on hours of presence at the office rather than outcomes achieved. Learning to reward attitude and behaviour first and outcomes second is essential. Attendance should have nothing to do with the reward system unless it impacts the team.

By rewarding attitude and behaviour, you can genuinely encourage the individual who motivates the team to be more performing, even if they are not personally as productive as desired. Some people demonstrate the skills listed here and are natural leaders, even if they don't have a position of authority.

17.3.9 Intelligence

Applying these principles requires a level of intelligence on behalf of management that is not traditional and certainly not taught within all the various MBA and other schools for future managers.

Intelligence, in this case, involves an interest in learning and understanding, an application of logic, and an ability to reason beyond traditional planning tasks.

Emotional intelligence is the foundation for compassion and other skills listed here. A manager also needs to demonstrate creativity and critical thinking in problem-solving.

Self-awareness is a great asset for the modern manager: being aware of your own shortcomings and limitations rather than continually seeking to demonstrate your skills and abilities. Your team members are perfectly aware of your idiosyncrasies, preferences, and faults – the more you try to hide them, the less you will be respected.

17.3.10   Knowledge

A consequence of intelligence and curiosity is knowledge. A good manager does not just know things but knows what is important and who is best placed to provide that knowledge.

The four most important steps to knowledge include:

- Understand what is important: what are the key facts and data that are critical to your team's success;
- Know what you know: understand the breadth and depth of your knowledge in various domains – don't pretend to know more than you do, but don't play the idiot when asking for explanations;
- Know what your team knows: be aware of the knowledge in the team, which team member is particularly adept in any given (useful) area;
- Know who knows what they need to know: facilitate the transfer of knowledge from the one who knows to the one who needs to know (through coaching, teaching, brain-storming and other methods).

17.3.11   Understand your Roles

As a manager, you have different roles to fulfil. You need to initiate projects and invite the right people to participate. Then, you need to protect your team: provide them with the information, the connections, the participants, the knowledge they need to do their work, and protect them from intrusive or disruptive external influences. Suppose someone wants to ask something to one of your team members that has nothing to do with their current focus. In that case, you should have a process to intercept that request and transmit it at the most appropriate time rather than allow an external person to break your team's concentration.

It would help if you regularly managed your position vis-à-vis the team: your place will change according to circumstances. You can have one of four basic positions with your team at any moment.

1. You are the spokesperson who needs to meet with customers, suppliers, senior management, and

others. When presenting the work accomplished by the team, you are the one who is managing the spotlight and shining it on the team to allow them to gather plaudits as appropriate.

2. You are a team member, "on the factory floor" with them when the pressure is on. You should never expect your team members to work longer hours than you do. When required, you should participate in discussions and negotiations with customers, suppliers, managers and others. You are a member of the team.

3. Oversight of the team is sometimes necessary for you to understand how the team is functioning, where conflicts might be simmering, or if reorganisation may improve the team's efficiency. There will frequently be one individual doing more than her fair share of the work – is this person a hero or a roadblock? How can you spread the workload more effectively (or should you)?

4. Finally, a crucial position, often forgotten or underestimated: you need time alone. We all need time to reflect and come to decisions and choices. Blocking a time for yourself regularly in your calendar, making sure that you have time during which no one will come and disturb you so that you can work on your own tasks, is critical at every level. Personally, I recommend blocking time for the whole team: give them a couple of hours every day during which no one is to be interrupted or disturbed, no emails or phone calls, just quiet work, each to their own. This simple habit will

rapidly increase the team's overall performance level[93].

17.3.12   Respect and Trust

Every good working relationship depends on respect and trust.

You need to earn trust and demonstrate respect.

To earn the trust of your team, you need to demonstrate clear ethics and be seen to maintain a healthy balance between business, personal and professional interests and priorities. You will have the opportunity to cheat and make decisions more beneficial to your personal advancement than that of your employer – consider these carefully and assume that they will be made public because they frequently are.

Your team members will not be able to trust you if you are not seen to trust them. If you are focused on controlling your team members, they will learn to work around your controls.

Managers who base their work around metrics (KPIs, OKRs and others) will soon discover that team members know how to provide data that makes their numbers look good.

If your focus is trust, your team members are more likely to trust you and do what is expected. But this requires demonstrating consistency and continuity in your actions

---

[93] An excellent book on the importance of taking time alone at work is Theo Compenolle's "BrainChains", which has the extensive subtitle: "Discover your brain, to unleash its full potential in a hyperconnected, multitasking world (Science About the Brain and Stress Explained in Simple Terms)"

and words.

17.3.13   Psychology and Sociology

We live in an interconnected world, and your work is no different. Your team and even you[94] are interconnected. You are a network.

Consider yourself and your team members as nodes of relationships rather than individuals. You are the meeting point of experiences, DNA and ancestry, education, studies, lessons learnt, accidents, encounters and more.

Consequently, each individual is unique and has insights, understandings and perspectives that are shared with no one else in the history of the universe. Respect that and seek to understand before you blame.

The same is true of your team: it is the combination of the individuals. That means your team is a node of nodes, a system of systems, a society of psychologies.

To manage the team, you need to listen and observe to understand what is important to the individuals and the team: what is holding this node together. Based on your observations, you should have the intelligence to decide how to respond to the team's combined needs, desires, skills and abilities. This should give you the ingredients necessary to adapt your objectives to communicate them so that everyone (including yourself) can adopt the approach that will bring success to the team.

Listen, respond, adapt, adopt

---

[94] As an individual, you might not be aware that more than half the cells in what you consider to be your body are not even human: you are full of microorganisms necessary to clean your pores, digest your food, and maintain your life forces.

Respect the wisdom of the team; it is the innate knowledge that allows them to react correctly to unforeseen events. Respect the team's instinct, the gut feeling: it forms the basis for the team's culture. Work within the culture, with the people you have.

Strengthen the way of working already in place, then allow or encourage variations that can be the team more effective. Listen to their experience, desires, complaints, and suggestions: they know what is not working correctly better than management.

Finally, pay particular attention to the sceptics, the naysayers. There are good reasons for them not to believe what you say will happen or is true. They are the ones who will identify the weaknesses in any plan you have to propose, and they are the ones you must win over.

18 Product Management

Within this document, I have focused primarily on establishing a quality culture. Naturally, quality is not achievable without some necessary documentation, practices and controls. Many models, theories and frameworks document these, so I will only review them superficially here.

18.1 Project Management

The concept of project management is to give a central person or team the necessary end-to-end view of progress and needs. This position allows the project manager to establish dependencies and relationships in time for resources to be available when needed.

> *Managing the project, not the people?*

The project manager is ultimately responsible for the project's success (from qualitative, budgetary, and timely points of view) but should not be directly involved in producing the results. The role is to plan, monitor, control, report and solve any issues that jeopardise the project's outcome.

Project Management is a series of planning and monitoring activities, not a job description. The Project Management activities can be performed by anyone who has been appropriately trained, or even several people if they are properly coordinated. Implementing a Project Management Office is one example of shared responsibilities and authority.

18.2 Requirements

No commercial activity should start without clearly understanding what the (potential) customers might want.

A traditional mistake in many organisations is trusting that customers really do want what they request, then being subsequently surprised to discover that the customer is unsatisfied with the resulting product or service[95].

It is essential to go beyond what the customer requests and start working towards what customers need rather than what they explain. To achieve this, you need to learn about your customers' business, what they are doing, and the priorities, developments and opportunities of their business, market, competition, and others.

18.3 Process Control

Some processes and standardisation are necessary to ensure the quality and reliability of the activities performed. Reliability and repeatability are needed to ensure that your customers can expect the same result, no matter which staff member is delivering the work.

Processes need to deliver value; the product of the process should always be demonstrably higher than the cost of implementing and performing it.

Processes are valuable. You need to ensure that people do what is necessary, complete the tasks in order, and report

---

[95] For more on this, see section 13.1.3 on "The Job to be Done" (page 83)

problems, deviations, progress and costs correctly. However, the process should be expected to outlive its usefulness at some point. It continues solving an old problem that no one remembers and never occurs. When this stage is reached, it may become excessively bureaucratic and need to be corrected, improved, or eliminated.

When performing a process definition workshop, I try to get the people doing the work to define their own processes. By discussing, designing, documenting and reviewing their approach, they are ready to accept and implement it. Their ownership of the process gives them the authority to change it when it proves unsatisfactory in practice.

A well-defined process must include:

- A clear definition of the desired outcomes or outputs;
- The list and status of all the components needed to do the work;
- Metrics and controls of the work in progress (rather than only having a control of the finished product).

18.4 Decision Analysis

Decision makers vary between wanting to give the appearance of basing all their decisions on facts and data while trusting their instinct[96]. Frequently, minor investments are analysed to death, while choosing to open a new office or move into a different market is made on a whim.

Of course, they will never openly admit to that.

Decisions are never entirely justifiable, and one has to

---

[96] I recently heard one well-known investor talking about how she "had a nose" for business and could always "sniff out" the problem areas.

trust personal experience, knowledge, instinct, preferences, bias, or whatever you want to call it.

On the other hand, it is unacceptable for the person making the decision not to take personal responsibility for the
choices made.

We all make mistakes, make bad choices, and we all fail[97].
Leadership and wisdom are found in accepting failures,
learning the lesson, and moving on.

Should a decision made in an organisation reveal itself to
be wrong, sufficient evidence must remain available to
identify the cause of the mistake. Lessons can only be
learnt if decisions are traceable and open.

18.5   Verification and Validation

Verification and validation involve checking that what
was done corresponds to what was initially requested (verification) and is usable in context (validation).

Every aspect of a business, every document, product, or
decision should be open to V&V. Sometimes, a 15-second
look-over is sufficient; other times, a thorough and
lengthy investigation and simulations prove necessary. If a
document is worth writing, it is worth having it checked
before it is made public. V&V cannot guarantee a defect-
free product but actively seeks to identify any defects that
would not be identified through other methods before fi-
nalising its subject.

Reviewing previous chapters, you will agree that thorough
V&V activities are necessary for mission and vision state-

---

[97] Joseph Conrad said, "It's only those who do nothing who make no
mistakes" (in *An Outcast of the Islands*, 1896)

ments, policies and processes, communication, and respect. Do not expect people to do something if you have not made an effort to verify that they have been informed and understood what is being requested of them. Do not expect compliance from people who do not know why something is important.

18.6 Risk Management

Every job should include a focus on risk identification. Risk management is the primary responsibility of anyone with some authority.

Risk management includes risks to projects, development work, business continuity, health and safety, environmental concerns, sales, education and training, and more.

There are hundreds of risks appearing every day; some of them are critical; some of them are too insignificant to demand your attention. Every risk should be identified and understood; a decision should determine what will be done in terms of mitigation and contingency[98]. One risk often missed is investing more resources in mitigating a risk than the potential resulting issue would have cost.

Risk identification involves encouraging all team members to look forward and seek out everything that might go wrong, and safely communicate risks without being accused of being disruptive or pessimists.

---

[98] Some risks have a very low probability and might easily be ignored, but their impact could be large enough to threaten business continuity – these should not be lost in the noise.

18.7 Supplier Management

Working with suppliers creates a new set of risks and challenges regarding quality and culture. By working with a supplier, you are handing over the *authority* for developing or delivering your product's quality to an external person or organisation while maintaining *accountability* for the result in your customers' opinion. If they get it wrong, your customers will come to you.

Therefore, you must always establish and maintain authority over that external supplier, controlling what they do, how they do it and whether you can improve their practices.

As a "prime contractor", you remain in control of the project at all levels and maintain the project management role. You establish and control the necessary steps in the supplier's requirements, design, build, integration and V&V activities.

A key strategy at this point includes a thorough and continuous effort of risk management and documented decisions.

19 Quality Is Not Standard

Vitruvian Quality is a concept that includes many different components and will take time to implement. It is not a standard, and I would never want it to become one.

19.1 We Need Standards

Standards are useful and can be critical to the success or failure of a business or even an industry.

Customers must receive an acceptable level of quality. When more than one person delivers services or builds a product, the quality level must be the same, not dependent on who does the work. You want to ensure that the product will not fail because it was assembled on a Friday afternoon. The employee showing up on Monday morning at a customer's site should not be hungover and dirty. And then there are more standards: the bolts you buy this year should fit the nuts you purchased last year.

Standards allow products to be consistent and predictable.

Other standards guarantee our safety: energy providers should be certified against ISO14001, the leading environmental standard.

So, while I will maintain that standards do not guarantee Quality, I do not want to reject the importance of standards. After all, I have penned two booklets on the intelligent implementation of ISO standards.

19.2   Standards Are Over-Rated

But many standards fail (or do not deliver the advertised results) due to their sales strategies.

Internal standards remain beyond their usefulness because they have become a habit. "We have always done it that way" "that's how our founding father said it should be". Instead of being a support, they become part of the bureaucracy and integrate the flawed principles of management by numbers.

External standards typically have the same history. Someone implemented a methodology in an organisation and was particularly successful. It was a good idea and achieved its objectives.

The originator gets the opportunity to try it in a different organisation and gets positive results again – this must be the ultimate solution.

With the help of a consultant, they sit down and write the book[99], give a TED talk, and promote the concept. It catches on, and more people implement it. So far, so good.

Then comes the next phase: there is big business in consulting and auditing.

Auditors come to check that you are doing it correctly. They don't understand your business and are not interested in it in the name of independent objectivity. Their approach is simple: if you do what the book says, that's good; if you don't, you fail. Consultants now take over: their job is to prepare you for the audit. Again, they are not interested in your business or customers. They are focused on

---

[99] Yes, I know, but I repeat: this is not a standard.

making sure you please the auditor. They will tell you what to do to pass the audit.

This is a lot of work. You need to give items the proper names, document things that everyone already knows, and make it look like what a lazy auditor might want to see. With all the additional preparation work, you have less time to focus on your customers, but that's for their own good, as the certification will prove worthwhile. Right?

You are now placing the proverbial cart before the horse. All the staff are putting in the effort needed to pass the audit[100]. When the auditor finally leaves the building, we can all be relieved and, finally, relax. The practices we were all pretending to do (for the audit) can now safely stop until next year.

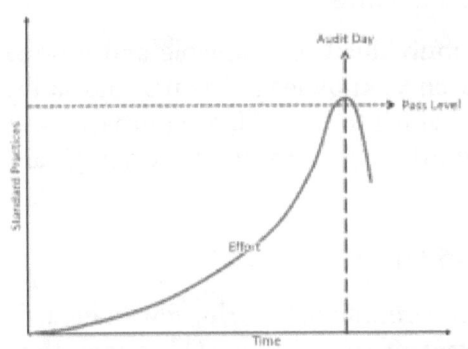

And that is how you get certified businesses making enormous mistakes, polluting the environment, getting their customer accounts hacked. "High Maturity" organisations deliver sub-standard products. Still, at least they are doing this predictably, repeatedly, measurably, and statistically consistent in their poor performance.

---

[100] I worked with one company that falsified and backdated so many reports for the audit, that it ended costing significantly more than if they had done the work correctly from the start, during the year. By doing it this way, they had more work over the year and none of the benefits of having done what they claimed.

19.3 The Foundations of Standards

Standards are based mainly on the principles of "scientific management", as defined by Frederick Taylor at the turn of the twentieth century.

> *"It is only through enforced standardization of methods, enforced adoption of the best implements and working conditions and enforced cooperation that this faster work can be assured."*

The paradigm that leads to standardisation is that people are factors of production. To maximise production, you must reduce variance and implement specialisation and formalisation. The best way to achieve that is to implement processes that allow comparative performance assessment and link this to compensation through targets and measurement of compliance.

My paradigm is that individuals are valuable and unique combinations of experience, knowledge, talents, and skills. Rather than locking them into a standard approach, you need to motivate them daily to improve how things are done.

19.4 Metrics and Evidence

Once released into the commercial world, few standards bother to gather metrics of their value. Of course, they have data to show you, they have books full of data. Only most of those data are irrelevant!

I have seen precisely the same data used by two very different standards to prove their value. Neither one of them was cheating. They both forgot to mention a vital component of every business seeking to improve: they do not limit themselves to one set of practices.

Businesses that are serious about improving try multiple approaches and standards simultaneously. They do not rely on the magic you read about or were sold by a consultant. If they are only taking a single standard as an approach, it is not to make things easier: it is because they are more interested in the certificate than the results. If they are only interested in the certification, their results and metrics are probably biased to prove their case.

> *No business serious about Quality will*
> *limit itself to a single approach*

19.5 Practically Speaking

As a manager or leader, everything you do should focus on ensuring that the people in your team have the means and the motivation to produce the Quality that will please your customers.

I have been asked several times for data and measurements proving that my recommended approaches work, and I am now going to disappoint all those who want the evidence. I have decided that I do not want to do that for several reasons. Some of which are explained earlier in this chapter.

In the past, I have worked as a process and quality consultant and coach for various standards. The experiences I used to create this volume come from various successful and failed improvement programmes.

I cannot guarantee a 15% increase in productivity due to Vitruvian Quality management. Just as no one can guarantee the value of implementing a standard like ISO, CMMI or Cobit.

When you measure something, you affect it, as we have

seen earlier in this volume. When you set a quantified goal, you subsume all other interests to one metric. You lose sight of the ecosystem in which everything is running.

Metrics were used to colonise the world, destroy the North American prairies, prove racial supremacy, justify eugenics, and so on.

Adolphe Quetelet was a Belgian astronomer who had a foundational role in creating modern statistics, including the concepts of correlation beyond causation. One of his discoveries was the constant murder rate in Paris: the number of murders remained similar, year on year. Even more spectacular, the proportion of strangulations vs stabbings vs shootings also remained constant. The publication of his analyses caused a debate about free will and whether there was any point in policing. Measurements are helpful, but they are often taken out of context and misused.

If you cannot believe me without evidence from businesses and organisations that have nothing in common with yours, I can't help you.

20 Conclusion

The main lesson to learn from here is that people develop Quality. It is not the processes, tools, or standards. Quality produces the business – not the advertising or the salaries.

Try my recommendations if you want. Don't if you don't. Do not believe that all your problems will be solved by doing precisely what I have said.

Try, listen, look, adapt, adopt.

> *It would be an unsound fancy and self-contradictory to expect that things which have never yet been done can be done except by means which have never yet been tried[101]*

Remember the maxims, as engraved on Apollo's Temple at Delphi[102]:

Know Yourself

Nothing to Excess

Surety Brings Ruin

---

[101] Francis Bacon in Novum Organum (1620). Quoted in "Beyond Measure: the Hidden History of Measurement", ©2022 James Vincent

[102] Γνῶθι σεαυτόν / Μηδὲν ἄγαν / Ἐγγύα πάρα δ' Ἄτα

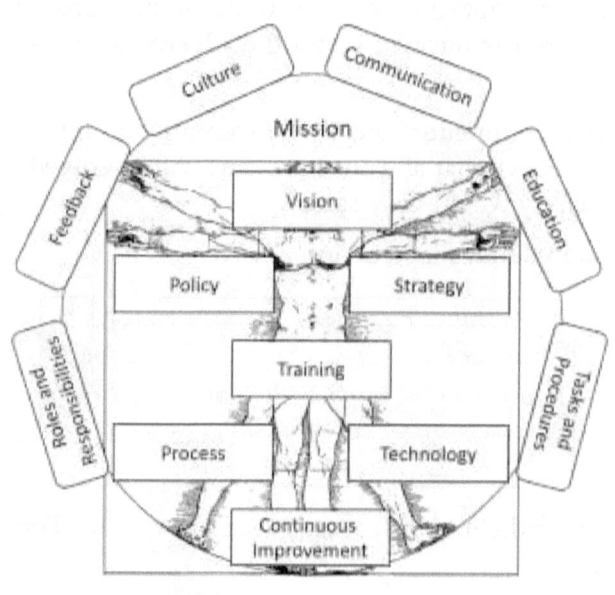